Butter Bread
Born-again:
I can only imagine

Amanda C. Ratliff

Creative Classics Publications US

ISBN: 978-1-7352724-8-1

Printed in the United States of America

This book is dedicated to those who might have grown up in challenging circumstances. Maybe without a father, a mother, or a family. Rest assured that your heavenly father has more love, wisdom, and power than you can comprehend. God is making a place for you in heaven. Thank you, Lord, for all of the miracles you have done in my life and all of the visions, dreams, and realities that you create for my family and me.

BUTTER
BREAD

Contents

Your sons and daughters will prophesy, your old men will dream dreams, your young men will see visions.
~Acts 2:17

Preface

Have you ever had a dream that was more than just a dream?

In mine, I was out in the desert, wandering around looking for a nail salon. I wondered: *Why would there be a nail salon in the desert?* but I knew I needed to keep looking. I found it and walked in. On the left I noticed two black, shell-shaped sinks, and to the right was a beautiful fountain that was bathed in bright gold and copper lighting. I could hear water trickling, and it was radiantly beautiful.

I walked over to the magnificent tub and sat down to put my feet in. Three other shadowlike people I didn't know were there—one on my left and two on my right, also sitting on the edge—with their pant legs rolled up and admiring the beauty. The feeling was unexplainable peace and joy. I noticed my bum was naked sitting on the side of the gold tub and wondered why but was astonished by this heavenly glow and peaceful joy all around.

We all put our feet in the fountain, and then I realized it was my son, daughter, and husband sitting next to me. All of a sudden, I slipped off the edge into the water. I heard everyone laughing, but it wasn't laughing at me; it was more of a heavenly, angelic laughter that I had fallen into the fountain. No judgment, no blame, just peace. I was smiling and laughing too because I had slid off the fountain so gracefully.

I looked over and saw a naked newborn baby in a circular basin inside of the fountain, which almost looked like an incubator ring with a light, and the baby's cooing, goo-gooing, and smiling—just so at peace. I was mesmerized watching how beautiful and innocent this baby was.

Then it occurred to me the baby's face was underwater, and it couldn't breathe. The baby was drowning, and in my dream I started to panic and became really distressed. *How can I save this baby?* At that point the baby propped itself up on its elbow and pulled itself out of the water.

As soon as the baby hit the air, I woke up, propped on my elbow. I lay there thinking: *Was that me? Was I just born, again?'* It was so vivid I knew it was more than just an overactive subconscious. I started to cry and laugh. My husband was getting ready for work and in a rush to get going, but I lay there a while to reflect on how radiant it all was. The black sink, the gold, the light—how serene, how pleasant.

Since that dream, I have often wondered if other people have had similar born-again dreams, as it talks in the Bible about being actually born-again. One of the first books I read growing up was a volume of *Chicken Soup for the Soul* that had stories where people talked about seeing angels and others like *heaven is real.* I was really captivated by those books and the idea of sharing these monumental, life-changing moments that were so inspiring and encouraging to others. But I had never thought about writing my own book until I had the rebirth dream, which was so profound. I felt as if I needed to cleanse myself from the past, logging the journey as my testimony to move closer.

Writing this book was hard in the beginning. Not just putting words to paper but also carving out the time between running my business and trying to really grow as a person. But as the weeks then months passed, I found myself gaining confidence, and a pull, a desire to write and document my journey to cleanse my soul. A greater comfort level occurred, and it became more like journaling.

I had a friend who once told me that after writing in her journal, she would rip the pages out and burn them because she wasn't writing to memorialize events but express her thoughts, and once expressed, she didn't need them on paper anymore. I do agree that writing is to get your thoughts out. But I also felt it wasn't just an exercise in expression to end up as ashes. As I wrote these chapters, I felt like I was growing as a person.

I did not grow up in the church. When I was younger I didn't give any thought to heaven or earthly spirituality. When I met my husband, his sister and he encouraged me to go to church, and I finally went. Her gentle and polite nudges to join her for weekend service led to life-altering moments. They say you never forget who led you to Christ, and I will always be thankful.

Looking back now I can vividly see the progression of how my life changed from before to after that decision. And even at the time, I felt the difference because my life was pretty awful at times during my "before Christ" stage, especially compared to the blessings that have come to me since. Through the theme of rebirth, I began to see the book as a chance to share my experiences, to connect with others who have traveled their own winding paths to Jesus. In this book I share my experiences and what being reborn in the spirit has meant in my life, with the hope that as you read, you'll reflect on what being of the spirit means to you.

At the same time I don't want to proselytize. I don't want to shove my beliefs down anyone's throat. I just want to share how my faith, how being born-again—in the fullest sense of the term—has changed, informed, and guided my life spiritually, personally, and even professionally, which leads me to the other purpose of this book. I want to offer readers a platform to share their own experiences by writing down their rebirth stories and submitting them on the *Butter*

Bread website. I want to hear stories about spiritual rebirth; has this happened to others? Are people born again? I want people to feel comfortable talking about these stories.

My goal is to create a series of books from these testimonies because I truly believe we should share our stories, visions, and dreams with one another and document each new victory just as they did in the Bible. We are living, breathing blessings created by him alone, and he wants us to share our testimony, our journey, no matter how hard. Through these stories we can build a community where we can both inspire and be inspired by one other each and every day.

According to the Bible, God continues to talk with us through dreams and visions, and we should be looking for them. Perhaps, when we have these dreams and visions, we are so close to him that we see how clear things really are. He talks in our ears. He corrects our thoughts. He begs us to be kind and say, *I'm sorry*. He wants us to walk in his foreverness of kindness and love. We must seek him and strive to be more like him. He wants us to be united in his glory and kingdom and almighty power. It's never too late.

If you would like to share your story of rebirth, send it to me either via TikTok or my personal email:
www.tiktok.com/@ButterBread333
Amanda_Ratliff@yahoo.com

Introduction

Imagine a rebirth. A clean soul. Being fully forgiven. A glimpse into the heavens. Realizing that we must endure sometimes unspeakable truths to pave the path to a new life.

Being baptized is a declaration that you have accepted the Lord as your savior and embrace him in every fiber of your soul. You commit to navigating away from sin and obeying his commandments, living each day in accordance with his Word and scripture to walk within his purpose. I believe allowing God to wash us clean of sin, provide healing, and bless us with forgiveness brings us closer to him and closer to being born again into the kingdom of God.

> *Very truly I tell you, no one can enter the kingdom of God unless they are born of water and the Spirit. Flesh gives birth to flesh, but the Spirit gives birth to spirit. You should not be surprised at my saying, 'You must be born-again' (John 3:5–6).*

As Christians we can question our holiness, our purpose, and whether Jesus is with us in spirit. I firmly believe he is always with us always, so once we are baptized, we are yoked with him in the spirit. The father, the son, and the Holy Ghost. We do not see him, yet we know without a doubt he is there. We have faith that he wishes only good things for us and that he is helping lead, guide, and direct.

1

Being born-again means letting the Spirit enter into us, so that I am led by the Spirit, not by myself, free, with this freedom of the Spirit, and you never know where it will end. ~ Pope Frances.

Being led by the spirit can be confusing. You may be unsure if you heard Jesus's voice—and did he really say *that*? We'll often ask for confirmation, clarity, or a sign, but trusting is key. On my daily walks I've learned it takes diligence not to be misguided. It's also taken me until this moment in my life to understand and accept the Lord sets the foundation. He has a time and a purpose. We must ask: *What does he want me to learn from this situation? Is there someone I am supposed to help?*

But once you embrace it, being led in spirit feels like the waves gently dancing at sea, the grass on the prairie, the cool breeze on your cheeks as you relax on a Sunday afternoon, or the smell of your favorite flower. It feels like you are catapulted into the unending and everlasting love of God, wrapped in strong, protecting arms and hearing the gentle whisper: *It's all going to be okay.*

As I approach midlife, I feel as though I'm just now finding who I am, allowing myself to know what makes me happy, to experience each day as a blessing, and learning how to experience happiness at each intersection of my life—to find joy in each moment. A quiet peace that can only be from him. We all need purpose, passion, or laughter. We all need to embrace time for ourselves. I find myself looking to write, paint, confide in trusted friends, reflect with quiet focus, exercise—these are all things that have supported my quest for healing.

Julia Roberts and Dolly Parton have become two of my favorite women. Their wit, charisma, charm, and quiet yet powerful confidence is something I've yearned for. Dolly, who I can relate to as a female entrepreneur, says that throughout her life, she's been imbued with the Holy Spirit.

"When I think I can't go on out that stage because I feel so bad physically, as soon as I get there, I just get lifted up in spirit and feel like I'm on that spiritual plane. And that's what I rely on. I always have, and I always will. And until God says stop, I'll keep going."

Julia Roberts converted to Hinduism in 2010 after she filmed the movie *Eat, Pray, Love*. She said it's drastically changed her life and provided spiritual satisfaction.

No matter what you believe or which religion you follow, one must believe that we are guided by spirits and living a supernatural life.

Sharing my story includes revisiting the depths of my past. I did not grow up knowing anything about spirituality, so for a long time I didn't know what it meant to follow Christ. I was intimidated by the Bible and the words written within it. I didn't know where to start. I'm hoping that newfound believers can relate to this sister who had to walk the same (often rocky) path to knowledge.

I was not able to see his beauty until I put him into focus. My hope is that by sharing my journey, you can begin to spot similar signs, visions, and wonders in your daily walk. As I relate the views and experiences I've had with Jesus, I hope that you can come to understand what it's like to live life *with* him. In this book I share what being reborn in the spirit has meant in my life—I have seen God completely change my life for the better.

As you read, please think about what being of the spirit means to you. I pray and hope this testimony will help you in your life and provide encouragement along the way.

Come near to God and he will come near to you
(James 4:8).

Chapter 1

Butter Bread Memories

It's estimated man has been eating bread for around thirty thousand years. Some historians even credit bread with playing a significant role in the development of ancient civilizations, as hunter-gatherers put down roots to start farming wheat and other grains.

Over the millennia bread has become a symbol of physical sustenance. So it's not surprising that bread was used as an analogy for our spiritual sustenance. In the Bible it has represented the relationship between God and the Israelites as well as Jesus and his followers. Paul even used the analogy of bread to describe the unity of believers as *being many we are one bread*. It would be a long time before I would see bread through a scripture's prism, so my earliest memories of bread were much more temporal.

Everyone has a childhood memory that brings an immediate smile to their face and surrounds their soul like a warm blanket. Perhaps waking up on Christmas morning to find your first bike under the tree. Maybe a family vacation where you experienced a moment of glee or contentment. As an adult I believe you can find Jesus and the joy he intends for our lives. As a child it was both soul-satisfying and delicious—butter bread.

When I was six years old, my best friend was Melissa, whose family had a large farm in Grove City, Ohio. They would work hard throughout the summer, tilling the land and shucking corn. They also owned a pizza shop, and in the summer Melissa's dad would take us to work with him, where we watched him flip and toss pizza dough in the air. To me each moment with their family was spectacular.

On the hottest of summer days, we would usually be in our bathing suits, spraying each other with the water hose and throwing water balloons. When we got hungry, we'd rush into her grandmother's house for a quick snack. Mrs. Sech would greet us with a smile. Her eyes were so warm. She had tight gray curls and was only about four feet tall—not much taller than us. Her usual outfit was hand-sewn, long sleeve blouses decorated with brown, white, and pink flowers, long denim skirts, and tennis shoes. A woman who embodied the meaning of living the simple life and caring for her family.

Melissa and I grinned with excitement as we sat at the kitchen table, waiting for her grandmother to set down a small serving plate piled high with six to eight pieces of perfectly buttered white bread. The rest of the loaf was open on the counter, ready for Mrs. Sech to quickly butter more, depending on how hungry we were. It was our favorite snack because it became a game, a race to see who could win. I remember pretending that Mrs. Sech had a checkered flag like at the beginning of a car race.

Ready, set, *go!*

We would shove as much bread into our mouths as we could. As soon as we could swallow without choking, we would shove another one and continue laughing in unbridled joy. Those memories are precious to me.

Today as an adult, I try to find butter bread moments in everything that I do because they cleanse your soul, and I believe it's what God wants for us.

> *And he said: "Truly I tell you, unless you change*
> *and become like little children, you will never enter*
> *the kingdom of heaven. Therefore, whoever takes*
> *the lowly position of this child is the greatest in the*
> *kingdom of heaven (Matthew 18:1-5).*

As a kid with Melissa, spontaneous joy came naturally. But within my own family, it became increasingly difficult for me to find as I grew older. It wasn't so much that I started to lose my way; it was more that I didn't know there was a better path waiting for me to follow.

Chapter 2

Family Impact

My mother and father were both Sooners, born and raised in Oklahoma, which is where they met and married, but they came from different backgrounds. My father's family was blue collar and my mother's white-collar. Although it made no difference to me at all, it did to others. My relationships with their respective families growing up were equally very different.

My mom's parents lived on a golf course. I remember them being well-heeled, always in dress shirts, slacks, and dress suits and quite involved in their community. They would host weekly card games and drink their favorite gin.

My grandpa, Papa Ron, who worked at NASA, helping develop and supply mission-critical materials, spent his free time solving crosswords. He was a warm-hearted man and always so pleasant. When you walked into their house, there was a large milk jug filled to the brim with quarters. As a little girl that fascinated me. Papa Ron would let us grab one handful of quarters. If any fell out, they had to go back into the jug, so we tried to make our hands as big as possible. It was a glorious memory.

My grandmother, Jeannie or Alice Jean, on the other hand, was not very kind to me. We were not close. Her tone, her gaze, and her stare all seemed unwelcoming, and I found her intimidating. Even as a kid I could sense she did not enjoy me and my personality, although she got along well with my sister, who was older, more outgoing, confident, and outspoken.

My most vivid memory was the day Jeannie was perming my older sister's hair in the kitchen. I excitedly asked her to perm my hair too. She declined and seemed very uninterested in me and preferred to dote on my sister. She died not long after that from cancer, so unfortunately, I would never get to know her at all or find out what was at the root of her hard-heartedness. I learned later as an adult that she'd been difficult with most of the people close to her, although I admit, I do not know the details—only how I experienced her for myself. I wish I could have let her know scars on your heart can be healed.

I will give you a new heart and put a new spirit in you; I will remove from you your heart of stone and give you a heart of flesh. And I will put my Spirit in you and move you to follow my decrees and be careful to keep my laws (Ezekiel 36:26-27).

My mother and father separated when I was very young, so I didn't know my dad's side of the family well. My aunt Linda and uncle Glen are amazing, I met them only once or twice when I was little but more so now as an adult. I only met Grandma Pat once that I can remember. When I was a teenager, my mother sent me to Oklahoma to visit her for a week. She was an absolute hoot and was very kind. She doted all over me and made sure I was well tended to during the trip. She crocheted me a special rose bedspread, which is still safely put away. She passed several years ago, and I wish I'd been able to spend more time with her. As with my maternal grandmother, the lesson learned is to try to restore relationships whenever possible; otherwise, you might have to wait until you meet them in heaven.

My paternal grandfather died when my dad was just nine years old so I never got to meet him. I'm sure not having his father around impacted my dad's life by not having that strong footing. So it's ironic that my dad left us when my eldest brother was also nine, perhaps an unintended generational pattern. I have come to know firsthand that generational patterns run through families. When my son was nine, my marriage also cycled through negative forms before I turned to Christ. The environment you grow up in becomes your known path. This is not a modern phenomenon; the Bible talks about generational sins. It's like we become hardwired to do unto others what was done to us, so you must make a conscious effort to break those patterns.

My dad didn't or couldn't. While his family was broken by death, ours was broken through divorce. My father had taken a bricklaying job in Mobile, Alabama, and was traveling a lot, working hard, and providing for the family. The travel created challenges, and my parents decided to end their marriage. It was heartbreaking for my brother and sister, but being the youngest I don't remember much about it. After my parents split up, my mother packed us up from Alabama and moved to Ohio. The only family we had there was an aunt and uncle. We would go to their house on weekends and holidays and watch TV, laugh, and eat popcorn. I had very fond memories, especially with Aunt Missy.

My relationship with my sister was never that close, so I often spent time annoying my brother. But being older, he always won those encounters. He once stuck me on top of a six-foot bookshelf, turned the lights off, and left opera music playing so loudly he couldn't hear me screaming to get me down. Another time I asked him what to do about my skinned knee, and he told me to put lemon juice on it, and I did—the curse of being the naive baby of the family. But those are memories I wouldn't ever change and gives us the giggles whenever it comes back up. My brother was always the life of the party and sought to bring peace and laughter in times of distress.

Once we moved to Ohio, I got the idea that I wanted a nickname. I was in the car with my mother one day when I asked her what a nickname was. She told me, then asked what nickname I would want. I was fascinated with Disney movies and had recently watched *Bambi,* and I'd been taken with the bluebirds in it that flew around Bambi's nose in one of the scenes. So I decided my nickname would be Bluebird. When meeting children from my new neighborhood, I'd tell them my name was Bluebird. My family started calling me that as well, and even today cherished friends and close associates call me Bluebird.

During that time I developed a very close relationship with my aunt Missy, who I loved—and still love—dearly. She was my confidant growing up. We would go out into her beautiful flower garden and talk about whatever was on my mind. I always admired her kind spirit and pure heart, setting aside time to always check in on me. She lives in Florida now, so I don't get to see her that often, but she has been a terrific friend and role model throughout most of my life and was a mentor when I needed it the most. But she couldn't save me from the cruelty of other children and bullies I encountered along the way.

Being raised by a single mom with three children meant we didn't have a lot. My mother worked several jobs to make ends meet. We sometimes ate a piece of bread with cheese for dinner or peanut butter and jelly sandwiches for dinner. Sometimes we had mustard sandwiches because that was all there was, and my mother was too tired to make dinner after a long day's work.

Even so, as a young child I was happy. We enjoyed the little things. We used to climb trees, play games, pick on our siblings, play tag, catch lightning bugs, wait on the ice cream truck, walk to the candy store, hang upside down on the monkey bars, and swing as high and as fast as you could. We would walk to school, do our homework, play all night, and get up without a care in the world. We were nothing but smiles. My favorite thing was sitting in the grass, picking four-leaf clovers—I still do that today.

Here is one of more than a thousand four-leaf clovers I've picked in my life. I place most of them throughout the pages in my Bible, and my heart melts every time I discover one in a perfect spot.

Adolescence was a different story, and the years from sixth to tenth grade were some of the most difficult times of my life.

Now that elementary school was over, I couldn't walk or ride my bike to school anymore, which was something I had enjoyed very much. Instead, I had to get up early and take a forty-five-minute bus ride to middle school, which was a complete culture shock for me. The district wanted to integrate and diversify different neighborhoods, so all our friends split and went to different schools.

Coming into middle school as an outsider, I was often the target of taunts. Up to then I had never been truly bullied, but starting in sixth grade I was bullied, harassed, picked on, and teased. It was an awful experience but taught me compassion for others. Years later one of my childhood friends from that time confided to me that she used to have her hair pulled and was even jumped. In talking with many other friends throughout the years, they shared similar incidents that happened to them. It could have been worse as many others experience abuse and other tragedies as children.

The verbal taunts were hard, and I learned to keep my head down. But being teased and ridiculed changed me and eroded my self-confidence and feelings of self-worth to the point where I felt *less than*. It also made me fearful and untrusting. I was unhappy at school and unhappy at home. I didn't have an outlet to share how I was feeling, to find comfort and direction. I didn't have God yet.

It was my natural inclination to sit in the front row and be the kid asking questions, wanting to learn more, soaking it in, and willing to help others. For that I was ridiculed, and it impacted my studies. I found myself underperforming academically because if I stuck out it made the bullying worse. Not that being attentive and participating seemed a requirement. My peers would get As just for coming to class, and they would often skip school to do drugs. The amount of cruelty I witnessed on top of being threatened on numerous occasions for no reason scarred and terrified me.

I changed middle schools three times before my mother got a small loan from her parents and purchased a house in a better school district. So in the eighth grade I was again one of the new students, with no confidence to strike up new friendships, especially since it felt like everyone had a clique.

But several special people made it a point to welcome me to the school, and I did make friends. Academically, though, I was totally behind the school curriculum, and I struggled significantly until I finally caught up my sophomore year in high school. Now looking back I can see that these experiences molded and shaped me to be more understanding and empathetic. It was similar to how Jesus was also outcasted in many social environments; he was punished for walking the straight and narrow road. Not that I can compare my walk at all with what our holy father experienced, but it paves the path of my journey to draw closer to him.

Once I adjusted to school, I might have been more on track with my studies, but I was veering off the rails between typical teenage hormones and not having any clear rules or boundaries about anything, including when and who I could date. My mother was very independent and worked hard to raise and support her children. And I didn't know what it was like to have a father or any strong male role model to let any suitors know he was keeping an eye on them.

For example, when my stepdaughter was picked up by a boy for their first date, my husband and his police buddies were all there wearing their service weapons, chests puffed out to roust the poor kid. But you can be sure he treated my stepdaughter with respect.

I didn't have that. And I made a lot of decisions I wished I hadn't as a teenager and walked into too many dangerous situations that I shouldn't have to keep up with my crew. I yearned for my earthly and heavenly father but didn't know that was the missing piece. I met my first boyfriend during this time and fell completely in love. I began to spend more and more of my time with him and stopped playing sports and attending afterschool events. I didn't make time for my friends and began to drift away from them. With no boundaries at home, I snuck out to be with him more times than I can count.

During sophomore year, my boyfriend started doing drugs. His behavior started to concern me, so we broke up, then got back together several times. When he started dating other girls, I tried to take my life by overdosing on medications and had to have my stomach pumped—not something I would ever wish on anyone. I was trying to find an escape, something to take my pain away.

My doctor diagnosed me with depression; interestingly, the medications he prescribed were found to have caused suicidal tendencies after later studies. Looking back, it makes sense, but I had no clue at the time why things were so rocky and unbalanced. I could never get the medications stabilized and was very shaky and emotional all the time. Through the mental fog I felt like I was in the depths of hell. I eventually stopped taking the medication and began to feel better. But I still needed *something*. It wasn't those pills at all, but I didn't know what it was.

Looking back now, I deeply wish that I could take those years back. I was deeply troubled, in some ways broken.

Even though I didn't know much about heaven or hell, I still worried about God's judgment of me.

But for as dark and depressing as that time was for me, it would give me perspective later in life. It also made me who I am. It's said that you have to experience adversity in order to grow, and there is no doubt I had so many things to learn about what *not* to do in life. I had to create my own guardrails about balance, control, optimism, and eventually trust in God.

I've come to realize that the devil wants us to live in shame, sin, depression, despair, and regret. He wants us to be afraid to admit to others and even ourselves that we are wrong. I know now that confession is a powerful tool. Talk to your friends, spouse, or significant other. I found out later in life that your pastor is also there for you to confide in. Talk to them. And if you can keep yourself surrounded by biblical believers and trust them, those are some of the most powerful relationships you will have. Cleanse your soul at every moment. The devil wants sin to be left in the dark. He wants to separate you from God and manipulate your weakest points. We need to begin to openly talk about the issues we have faced so we can all learn and be held accountable.

What I can see clearly now is that as a teenager, I didn't value myself, and I lacked confidence, so no surprise this experience with my boyfriend left me with deep-seated trust and abandonment issues that would impact my relationship with my husband and males in general for many years after.

~ Chapter 3 ~

The Importance of Sticking Together

I often feel that we don't appreciate the importance of family nearly enough or acknowledge how much we need them to encourage and strengthen us. While I loved my family, as a teenager it didn't give me quite the guardrails I needed. An important aspect of adolescence is testing limits, but you still want a safety net of boundaries, so you don't go into freefall if you misstep. After making it through high school, even though my confidence and self-worth were still a bit bruised and battered, I was looking forward to a new chapter. What my life going forward would look like was still to be determined, but I knew it wouldn't include going off to college, at least for the time being. There was no way I could afford to go full time.

My mother tried to nudge me toward healthcare, which was her industry. But to me that was a non-starter as I was not initially interested in it. So in the summer of 1999, I went to work at a local bank, starting off in finance. I loved the math and serving the customers.

I was very precise with cash balancing and made sure everything was perfect. All of the dollar bills had to be facing the same position, and I counted and recounted everything multiple times. I was the anal-retentive employee who noticed if anything was misspelled or out of place. The bank promoted me to vault and ATM teller, and having that responsibility for all those deposits was very gratifying. Counting money and making sure everything was balanced was definitely my thing. My mother used to joke that when I was in elementary school, and the gym coach said to run a lap, I would run twelve. I might have been introverted, but I was also competitive and strove for perfection. I want to be the best in whatever I'm doing.

I was a typical young professional woman with my own apartment, bills, and responsibilities. That time in my life—being independent and growing into my own—was a lot of fun. I worked hard, spent free time with my girlfriends, took walks in the park, blasted music in my car, drew art, and learned glass making.

On an evening out with my childhood best friend—a Friday the thirteenth—I met my future husband when I was twenty. I was at a small country bar and saw him line dancing in his cowboy hat and boots. I was mesmerized because I can't dance worth a lick. I must have watched him for hours that night; he was having so much fun.

One of my friends saw me eyeballing him, so she walked over, pulled him over to our table, and introduced us. He took his cowboy hat off.

"Hi, my name is Andy."

My heart skipped a beat, and we spent the rest of the night talking, laughing, and dancing. To this day my friend takes credit for our marriage, saying *You would never have married him if it wasn't for me.* And I probably wouldn't have. I was an introvert, and he was clearly more extroverted and was no doubt a jock in high school. So no, I would have never gone up to him.

Andy and I soon started dating. Then we were a couple, and he gave me a promise ring after six months, which I thought was the sweetest thing ever. But we didn't get married right away. I wanted to make sure that I knew

Andy's family—his upbringing and the situation with his ex-wife, with whom he had a daughter—and really understood who he was before we bit the bullet.

I quickly learned the differences between my husband's family and mine were night and day. My parents divorced when I was very young. From what I understood, the relationship between Andy's parents was rocky early on, but as they became older, they fell more in love and were married for more than thirty years.

Andy grew up Southern Baptist, so his family spent *a lot* of time in the church, and his aunt was an evangelistic minister. While not atheists or agnostics by any stretch, my family was not church-going.

I knew a few scriptures but wasn't active in the church. I didn't see my mom praying, reading, or reaching out to Jesus. Maybe she did it discreetly, quietly, and in her own time. There was an eagle picture that she had hung with scripture that got her through troubled times. The picture was the only thing left in a random army barrack her friend had let her stay in during her trip to Ohio when she left my father. It read:

> But they who wait for the Lord shall renew their strength; they shall mount up with wings like eagles; they shall run and not be weary; they shall walk and not faint (Isaiah 40:3).

Seeing eagles was her sign from the Lord, so we would look for them wherever we went. But beyond that I had no clear understanding of who God was, nor had I really ever questioned anything about it. Maybe I wondered how the stars and universe was created but not in any spiritual sense.

But this difference in religious upbringing wasn't a deal-breaker, and after several years of dating, we got married on April 13, 2005. Since we had met on a Friday the 13th, we planned our wedding for that day and went out to Las Vegas for the ceremony. No, it wasn't one of those Elvis wedding chapels. It was at the Valley of Fire state park in Odenton, Nevada, which is known for its beautiful red rock.

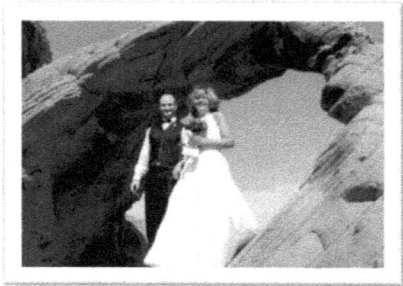

It was a simple affair. We rented a limousine, which took us from the Strip out to the desert. I bought a $99 David's Bridal dress, which was absolutely gorgeous. My sister, a florist, made me the most beautiful tulip bouquet I took with me on the flight. Tulips were my favorite flower. My dad and my aunt Joyce came and took all of the pictures. It was simple, fun, and the most memorable experience because we did it on our terms.

We were there for a week enjoying the honeymoon, playing a few slots, and walking around to tour the shows. We actually ended up winning $1,300 on a rogue $1 bet that my dad insisted we play on our way out the door. When we got home, my mother did a barbecue at a local park with dancing and cake as a kind of reception for friends and family. We had about 125 guests, and many of our friends came in from different states, and our favorite teachers were glad to attend.

In the first year or so, we moved several times, from an apartment to a townhouse to a house that was walking distance to a nice nondenominational evangelical church, Vineyard Columbus. Andy's sister Veronica kept inviting us to that church. *Hey, we're going to go on Saturday night, please join us.* I kept resisting. I think because it was the unknown. I knew there was something bigger than me, but I didn't know enough. And when I opened the Bible, it was intimidating.

But one day Andy nudged me and said, "Let's go."

The pastor, Rich Nathan, who has helped grow the Vineyard Movement, was thought-provoking and very charismatic. I became less resistant about going to church but was still in the early stages of finding my way. Over time, though, I would experience instances of God's grace that would start breaking through my defenses.

I didn't really know what it was like to have a father until I met my husband's father, Bob. I really looked up to him and developed a strong relationship with him. At every holiday he was such a joy and brought so much laughter. Bob got very sick, and as he got closer to death, we began visiting him nearly every day, helping the family take care of him at home on hospice. One day he wanted to go to church! The whole family went that day. I watched him during the service as he raised his hands to the sky and wept tears to Jesus. He wasn't able to stand, but he was filled with the spirit—no pain at all—and had unwavering hope at that moment.

Seeing the light in his eyes, in his heart, how he was moved by the spirit of God's grace and compassion was the first time that I felt *something*. Since Bob was so important to me, I wanted to get closer to God. In that moment, I thought: *I need that. Whatever it is, I need it.*

My mother-in-law became a widow in 2006. She never remarried and to this day holds Bob as number one in her heart. After my father-in-law died, I struggled tremendously. It was like I had lost my own father all over again. I wanted to be there to support my husband but was so overcome with my own grief that I acted out. I began to resist our marriage. The devil was trying to push himself in, and I was resisting God. Our marriage was no fairytale and was about to get rockier.

Around the time I gave birth to our daughter, the housing market dropped as the Great Recession hit, so Andy didn't have work for months. Money was so tight I had to go into Kroger and beg the manager for Similac to feed our child. It was so embarrassing. I was hoping they would donate groceries, but they gave me two cans of formula, which was nearly $50, and it felt like a miracle at my lowest moments of despair.

Vineyard Columbus had announced financial counseling support with Dave Ramsey tools and help for those impacted by the recession and ended up providing us aid. The church stepped in and helped Andy with his résumé to apply for jobs, provided financial coaching, and gave us $1,000 to pay our rent. In that moment I saw firsthand the humility and blessings that God's Kingdom could provide. It was an amazing feeling to have them help and come along side us.

Things were still rough raising two young children on a one-income household, but we were being tested, transitioning from caterpillars to butterflies. I was very young in my walk with my faith, but between having seen the love of God in my father-in-law's face, the polite nudges from my sister-in-law, and then that boost from the church during a difficult time, I was ready for a change. I surrendered. At that point in my life, I felt like God had met me where I was. And he began to show up with little miracle moments.

Despite the help from the church, we were struggling financially but we had hope. We began to see the joy come out of such a dark period. Andy had now been out of work for three months, and for a while we had to get government assistance to buy food and Medicaid to provide our medical care. It was hard to see how we'd dig out of the hole we were in.

Then one day the hot water tank exploded and flooded our entire kitchen. We were so discouraged, having no idea what we were going to do. It was the dead of winter, and there wouldn't be any work for Andy until the spring. I was so upset that our kitchen was ruined by the flood. But what seemed like yet another catastrophe turned out to be a ray of light through the clouds.

The adjuster came, and our insurance wrote us a check for $20,000 to fix everything, which Andy could do himself. The excitement on our faces at that moment was unexplainable. That check was a lifeline. Suddenly we had $20,000 in the bank, enough to fix our outdated kitchen, pay our mortgage, and buy groceries. We did not have to use a contractor, and as long as we submitted the receipts, the insurance would cover the expense. It was truly the miracle we'd been praying for.

Sometimes God sends storms to clear the path, and this was the moment I saw firsthand how unbelievable he could be, my first testimony of God's unwavering devotion to me, to us. For the first time I recognized a blessing from heaven and thought: *Thank you, Lord.*

Then it was like God wanted to double his portion and see our surprise again at what an awesome God he is. He wanted to impress upon us that he was the provider. That miracle turned into another. When the insurance agent was inspecting our kitchen, he was very thorough and looked under the crawlspace and found another $5,000 worth of damage from a leaky pipe that he estimated had been leaking for a year. We had no idea, and it had soaked the floor above. With that report, we were able to get a $600 credit on our water bill, add some much-needed funds to our account and get new floors in throughout the house.

This was right before Christmas, so we used a little bit of the money to buy used clothes and games from Once Upon a Child to give to the children at Christmas. A Christmas miracle. Then while out at a local thrift store, a woman came by and handed me an envelope with a beautiful card of a Christmas angel—and $250 cash. I wept right there with my infant daughter Gabby in the cart.

Bless your Holy Name, Jesus! But he wasn't done.

The very next week, a large hailstorm came through our area and damaged our roof, qualifying it for brand new shingles. It was over $8,000 for the roof, and because my husband knew the vendor, we were able to get it at a discount and save the rest to pay down medical debt. After these multiple miracles our house and our family were in better condition than we could have ever done on our own. I believe God gave us that money for six months so my husband could provide for us and help us get back on our feet.

Mind you, I had to do the dishes in the bathtub for about three months, but I was not about to complain. God had shown up with a new kitchen, a new floor, a new roof, and income for our family at our most desperate time. The circumstances had looked so grim for us, new parents trying to make ends meet, and God showed up. I was convinced; God had moved me with his power. I believed.

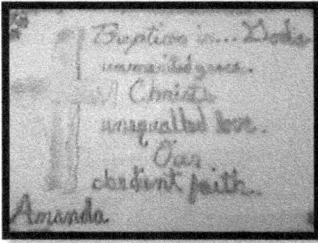

But I did not consider myself a Christian until June 21, 2009, when I was baptized. The church had announced a baptism on my birthday, and I had to do it. My husband couldn't attend because he had decided to change careers and was in training at the police academy. He was so apologetic, but I understood because he was still there in spirit. Many of our Bible study friends and all of our family showed up to support me—one even made me a cake. I was honored to be a part of God's team. It was the most loving feeling I had ever experienced. Acceptance and love—I was finally home, a child of God, all of my blemishes put to rest.

I must proclaim with all my soul that God is real. I've seen it with my own eyes time and time again. Thanks to my sister-in-law gently nudging us to go to church with her, even though I rejected the invitation many times, I eventually went, and it changed my life because it opened me to miracles. So don't resist God. Belief changes your perspective and makes clear the path you need to follow, even if you occasionally take a wrong turn. It informs every aspect of your life, every relationship, both personal and professional. I cannot imagine life without him.

This is not to say that life is suddenly a daily picnic with all struggles magically gone. But it does mean you have the ultimate source of strength when going through life's challenges—and for me there were many more to come.

~ Chapter 4 ~
# New Career Direction

After working at the bank for almost five years, I left there in the summer of 2004 to work full time at Aetna. Yes, despite all those years adamant I wouldn't end up in healthcare, sure enough I ended up at a healthcare company, working in customer service and claims. A couple of years later I joined Molina, and during my time there, I worked my way up to a senior contract specialist and helped build one of the initial startup Medicaid plans in Ohio. I really loved Molina's cultural vibe; we were all family and looked

out for one another. And my husband had now left construction and become a full-time police officer, a career move that completely changed his life.

By 2008, we had a new daughter, a seven-year-old son, a nine-year-old daughter, a lovely home, and secure jobs. Things were going well, and we were embedded in a strong small group. But I decided to take a new position at work. And that's when the devil stepped in. I was traveling out of state a lot and only flying home on the weekends. For a six-month period, I was often gone three weeks out of every month, with my husband working the third shift. My mom was watching the children overnight, but we were missing our routine and our church. I thought the sacrifice was worth it, but my work demands put increasing stress on me and my marriage. I let the darkness creep back in as I was recovering from having a baby. I started to want more in life and was likely suffering from postpartum depression and threatened to leave our marriage. It was a very rough patch for us both. My hormones were a mess, and we were tired and grumpy with each other. Because we were not going to church, we were fighting more than usual. We lacked our routine, and I wasn't home.

Looking back now I'm ashamed of how I treated my family, that I wasn't there, and that I let us get out of our pattern. I was tired and easily upset. The house was always a mess, and I missed my family so much from the travel and not being able to be home with them. How easily I slipped with my devotions and time with God. I stopped going to church, stopped small group, stopped reading the Bible—everything. The devil had control of me and pulled me away from his glory. I started to think it was easier to give up on my marriage than to stay. I wanted to give up on everything.

If it's not working, time to throw in the towel, I told myself. That is what I was used to, and it was so easy to fall back into that pattern. In retrospect I now see that I had no idea what a marital commitment was, no true understanding of the *for better or for worse* vows I took, no appreciation for the true meaning of love. The scars from previous boyfriends and an absent father made me want to flee. I was self-sabotaging. No doubt the devil was lurking during that time, which can make anyone stumble, challenge any marriage. We needed God more than ever; we needed to live in the light instead of the darkness.

As I began to reflect on the situation, I noticed a pattern. Our son was around the age of nine when I wanted to escape—the same cycled pattern as my dad's dad left him at nine. And my dad left my brother at nine. I wondered if I was perpetuating a generational pattern. It was an odd thought, but if it were true, I needed to do everything I could to break it. I suddenly felt like I needed to protect our family. Andy was both a friend and loving husband during that time for me. I believe now that God had united our souls to teach me what marriage was. We needed each other. He wouldn't let me just give up; that's too easy.

Look around in your life and see if you've got a group of friends or loved ones cheering you on, telling you when you're wrong, or encouraging you when you're on a positive path. You need to have the right friends, peers, and believers who trust in him to help pull you back when you're wrong. We must admit our failures and weaknesses to strive for better. It's accountability.

We should council and check in. Help each other wear off the rough edges. Pray and worship together. Go to church routinely and talk to our pastor when things get rough. We are meant to do life together. I would not be here without my husband, friends, and church family rooting me on. We can't be in a community from our living room, watch church on an iPhone, or sit in isolation. Being together, admitting our faults, and holding each other accountable, helps us stay on a healthy spiritual and emotional path.

Part of my fresh start and reset was resigning from Molina because all the national travel was too hard on my family. So despite rejecting the idea for years, I went to work for my mother at her company. I was nervous to work for family, but I knew I could make a difference. My job was in the healthcare service administration of the company's post-acute care network. My goal was to help grow her business, which supported nursing homes and home health agencies.

In addition to working full time overseeing operations during the day, in my off time I also established my own company, ARC Healthcare, to offer contract management, provider data, directory consulting, enrollment, and reporting, among other services. Simply put, my idea was to help health plans by supporting their business processing.

I've always been an entrepreneur at heart because wherever I worked, I never wanted to be put in a box. I wanted to be the one always forward-thinking, and I got that from my mother because she's a real go-getter. I worked on the startup part-time during the evening and on weekends for several years, getting small jobs here and there.

My mother knew I was working on it and was fine with it, especially since it did not affect the work I was doing for her. And when I secured a small contract for staffing eight people, she let me borrow some space in her office and was running that on the side. That contract validated my belief that ARC had the potential to really grow.

While things were okay professionally, it's no secret that working with family brings unique challenges. I had ambitions for my job and gave it my all, but over time it became too personal. When I tried to show my mother some ideas to improve her business systems or processes, she was resistant to my advice, which bothered me both as an employee and as her family member.

Did being her daughter prevent her from seeing me as a professional peer? Maybe. Whatever the reason, I had to build barriers around that because I wasn't being heard. On the other hand, it was her company, and she wanted things done a certain way, which I had to respect. Still, it became clear that we had very different management philosophies.

Beyond that, our relationship lines were getting murky. Like when we'd go to Christmas holidays or get together for family gatherings, she would be talking about work. And I would think: *This isn't what I want for the rest of my life. I want my mom to be my mom.* I saw I needed to commit to a new professional path. I needed to use ARC Healthcare as a way forward and not treat it like some side hustle. While change can be scary, it can also be liberating—as well as a chance to walk the spiritual walk.

Chapter 5

Faith-Based Workplace Culture

After some prompting from a dear friend, I left my mother's firm and started to grow my own business. After ARC Healthcare was awarded two small contracts, I sublet a small office and needed to hire about a dozen staff. It was an exciting time, buying new computers and equipment and decorating my new office for client meetings. I wanted to weave in crosses to remind me of who had led me to where I was, to be a constant reminder for me to keep me engaged.

I understand that faith is a personal journey, and I don't ever want to force my beliefs on anyone else. That said, I wanted to run my business based on the principles, ethics, and belief system that are rooted in my faith. And I made the decision early on to be open and upfront about it. I learned that wasn't always a popular path to take.

To be honest, I had wanted other employers to be more outspoken about Christ in their businesses, but many weren't willing to do that. How do I build a culture like Chick-fil-A, closed on Sunday? I asked my uncle what his thoughts were.

"You could lose a lot of people by being so outspoken," he once warned me. "You've got to remain bipartisan."

While I understand his point, this is who I am. I want to be bold and talk about Christ, and I want people to see him in what we do at ARC: how we treat and respect our vendors, clients, and employees; how we conduct ourselves in business. I believed if I were true to myself, I could be both a successful entrepreneur and ambassador of God.

Because of that I felt it was important for prospective employees, whether a stranger or someone I already knew, to understand that. So as the company grew, at times I would do personnel interviews because I wanted people to hear my voice. I wanted people to see the vision and the passion and understand where I was trying to get to. But I wanted to make it clear that we didn't discriminate based on religion or any other factor. And I wanted to see what vision the applicant had for their future, what their goals were so I could help them get there. The business was built on faith and the foundation of God. It was important to me to ensure that employees were successful. I'd ask where they wanted to be in five or ten years and what kind of work they like to do because putting your team somewhere that they're not happy is not a recipe for success.

For example, I'm not outwardly focused. At a conference you wouldn't find me in the forefront saying: *Hey, come talk to me.* I'm not that person. Now, there are people who would argue that from their perspective, I'm quite extroverted. But I'm naturally introverted, and I prefer being behind the scenes. That's my sweet spot. So for me as a boss, it's about finding out what people strive to do and where they want to be to make sure that they're content in their job.

And while I obviously do hire people I don't already know, I'm a big believer in hiring people you do know, especially when you're just starting out. I think when you build a business that's so personal, you have to bring on friends who meet the qualifications because they come with built-in trust.

I know some people disagree with that, and some have criticized me about it, but to me it's meaningful to build on relationships. That's important for a stable foundation. I'm all about having a family dynamic at the core of company culture. It creates a good environment for employees that in turn lets us provide the best service possible. Many other businesses are the same. But weaving in Christ is usually for non-profit churches and companies like Hobby Lobby. I believed it could also be viable for a small, woman-owned business. On our website our core values are also front and center:

Ethical
To be good stewards of state and federal dollars
To conduct business with the highest level of integrity
To achieve excellence through effective quality controls

Dynamic
To be a team that makes positive impact
To be in pursuit of perpetual knowledge
To lead by example and inspire others

Committed
To our client' goals and objectives
To serve the underprivileged, and to show love and respect at every intersect
To help and advocate for women and minority-owned business

Trustworthy
To have a collaborative team
To work with desire and determination
To produce deliverables with pride and honor

From the get-go everyone who comes to work with me knows the culture. It's in our handbook that the business is faith-based. I tell people upfront we pray, we laugh, and we cry together. Christ is very apparent in all that we do because he is the author and the creator. I don't want to go where he isn't leading.

I need to have very visible signs of Christ, such as crosses in the office and such. God is my rock, guide, and innovator. I want to forewarn new employees so they know what they're stepping into. I want to make sure they are part of the success and journey. You need to make choices to ensure your passenger list is in concert with both your journey and destination. And I realize not everybody is suited for or comfortable with my company's faith-based foundation.

The qualities I wanted in the individuals or businesses I worked with, namely integrity, honesty, and respectfulness. If you're not treating my team and me well, it's probably not going to work. We need more unity, understanding, and inclusiveness in our culture. In my opinion God put us all here to work together cohesively.

Not everyone takes kindly to that belief. I've had some harsh things said to me. One person told me that I *over Jesusfied* the office. It just didn't make sense to me. If you're somebody who really enjoys Christ in your life, how do you *over* Jesusfy it? So I've had to swim upstream.

But then I've always gone against the grain. And that's true with how I've built the company as well. I have never really focused on growing the business—that's up to God. I just wanted to invest in the bigger vision over the long haul. I trusted growth would be a byproduct of that, of taking the time to establish relationships with clients, and treating them with the courtesy and respect they deserve. This is God's business, not mine.

My role is to honor and respect the employees and the customers. It's like the old saying: you can catch more bees with honey than vinegar. I grew up in the South, and it's really important to me to always say *Yes, ma'am* and *No, sir* and be respectful because, at the end of the day, it all comes down to how you treat people.

Am I perfect? Not even close. I have days when my patience is in short supply. There are times I'm not as considerate or as thoughtful as I should be. God doesn't expect perfection. But I believe he does demand honesty. So I always try to own up to it when I fall short. If you mess up, say you're sorry. Acknowledging your error goes a long way with people. Things go awry sometimes; such is life.

At the end of the day, I believe you need to have a Christlike attitude in how you treat people in your day-to-day life, and we strive to show that in our overarching company culture. As success continues and as we grow to scale, we need to ensure that we get all communications on point and have everybody in the right roles as one united team. Once all was aligned, then it was making sure we didn't fail because failure was not an option.

Things were good for a couple of years, and then I hit a lull. I prayed to God to help me keep my team employed. I didn't want to let anyone go. And God blessed us with a billing opportunity. The contract was exactly enough to cover payroll for three months. God had seen a way through. I made no profit, but it got us through until we were awarded additional business.

During that time, I prayed harder than I had ever prayed before. We were then awarded the largest contract yet and scaled from twelve employees to over two hundred people in less than thirty days. That account gave me the ability to acquire the best teams and infrastructure needed for long-term growth. God had told me that I needed a good COO, and she was placed *right in front of me.* She was so perfect that I hired her on the spot, and she showed up the next day to corral the team and start planning for our training and orientations. God gave me the very tools I would need to succeed. Every member of my team was hand selected by God, and to watch how he puts things together so seamlessly is miraculous.

As a result of the new contract, I decided to rent a beautiful old house, and a wonderful friend named Mary offered to help decorate it at no charge. It was a beautiful blessing. Once she was done decorating, she asked if I had

Ratliff

a favorite verse so she could display it at the entry of the door. I told her that I didn't, so she opened the pages of the Bible directly to Esther, and she said that 4:14, which talks about how God will have his way and accomplish his purposes—"perhaps you were born for such a time as this"— spoke directly to where we were in that moment.

As she selected things to display throughout the office, there were visible signs of God's presence, reminding me that he was near. The white lace curtains had a little clover pattern, which was the logo for a customer life cycle management tool we were implementing. The two pictures we chose from a local antique market, out of four hundred other pictures, had our company name on the back. It was too surreal that God was reminding us of his promise and that our journey was real.

Mary is a true woman of God and a blessing sent from heaven. I would literally be nowhere without her kindness and willingness to help, no questions asked. She stepped in and was there with words of encouragement and hope when I needed them the most. I was so tickled by her spirit. She is such a delight and doesn't even know how much this one moment changed so many lives. Without her push with that key verse, I would not be where I am today.

Good thing because the work was challenging, and I wanted to cry every day. And in fact I did cry most days because we were being challenged. We were hiring, scaling, punching numbers, securing equipment, setting up, developing systems, training people—it was a lot. But it was fun. Implementing new things and operations is where I belong. I was being tested and growing within myself personally and professionally to prepare me for more. A friend shared this scripture with me. It is through perseverance that we must continue with the Lord.

Those who plant in tears will harvest shouts of joy! (Psalm 126:5).

I have no doubts that whatever success my company has had is because I braced myself on a firm foundation of biblical attitudes and the favor of God. That is not to say it's all been smooth sailing with everyone singing "Kumbaya." I wanted to give up at the end of every day, but each new morning brought new energy to resolve. I wanted nothing more than to serve my customer and bring satisfactory results. I was on a journey for God, to bring solutions and provide jobs in my community.

I think the way we live right now in our culture makes people shift around in their seats a little bit uncomfortably when you talk about faith, so we need to be bold with it, without being draconic about it, without being political about it. Everyone has a point of view; listening is imperative.

Yes. I would rather fail at this one thing than forsake my own belief. I'd rather lose everything, look back, and say it was a fun ride based on me putting Christ in the center rather than knowing I didn't do that. But that doesn't mean I expect others to be at the same place on their journey that I'm on in mine on a faith level. But I do expect anyone working for me to be respectful, caring, and compassionate toward everyone they deal with.

Every day I choose to put Christ in the center of *my* path, and I'm going to follow the direction that he tells me. There's no doubt that he's guided me here through every tear, every conversation, every new client call, every bill that's due, all the payroll—everything.

Every day I hear a word from him: *Go do this. Go talk to that person.* It's like divine navigation.

And sometimes when he talks, I'm not always sure what he means. I spend a lot of time outside, and I enjoy doing yoga prayer at dawn, watching the sun come up. One morning back when the company was still establishing itself in the industry, I was sitting there in the lotus position, trying to figure out who my strongest leaders were in the company. *Who would best help me build a solid foundation for the business so I could scale?*

Then God said: *Pick up these rocks.* So I did and arranged them in a circle in front of me. I began trying to stack them from top to bottom vertically, they started to form a team but kept falling over. Well, trying to balance those eight rocks vertically was not as easy as it might sound, and they kept falling down. I started getting frustrated because it wasn't working.

Then he said: *Pick up that one*, which was shaped exactly like a mountain. Then he told me to try and stack them. He said: *Instead of trying to stack them all on top of each other, to go around the mountain. Put this in the center, and now try to stack them.*

So I took the rocks and began to overlay them. It *worked*. There was a strong base, and the rocks started stacking much better as they were piled around each other, vs. top to bottom. Then I had a smaller stack below this other grouping. This direction is only something you can experience with God—divine instruction.

The next thing I know a baby centipede comes along to check things out and doesn't go through or over. He goes below the rocks and then around my bottom. He wanted to go under me—literally waited until I pulled myself up so he could go under. I had to raise up so he could go under. Then the centipede preceded to do it again. He did two full circles, and I asked God what this was about.

He said: *This is your team. You cannot build your organization chart straight up and down; your team needs to be around you.*

He gave me the leadership team in this vision. The exact names of those I had to hire to support us. The smaller rocks were the rest of the management team, and then the centipede was the rest of the organization. He said: *You have now created this team that will carry you. They will **lift you up** and **run circles around you now**.*

It was the most awesome experience I have had. I cannot even explain in words the sketch he visually laid before me. Time and time again God finds a way to speak to us. He tells us where to move, how to move. God even directed the little centipede to show me the path.

I took the rocks, bagged them, and have them in my office today. And he was right; my team was rock solid, and so was the foundation of the company. First and foremost our emphasis is on treating others with respect, and I believe it sets my company apart from most of the competition.

That and honesty, integrity, and being able to step back and say: *I feel proud of what I'm delivering.* I always try to put myself in my customers' shoes and think: *If I were on the receiving end of my service deliverable, would I be a happy customer? If I give my word, is there transparency? Can I feel right about what I'm billing, what I'm saying or doing, or how I'm delivering it?* I cannot lie or steal. I mean, I cannot even walk out of a store with a bag of potatoes on the bottom of my cart that I didn't pay for without going back in to pay the $2.99 for them.

As a company grows, there can be challenges in maintaining the purity of the culture we've established because if you hire someone who turns out to be a bad fit, it can have a ripple effect. A negative and dishonest employee can ruin reputations. But God told me something a few years ago before the pandemic that I find interesting. He said *my company was going to grow sixteen rungs from where we were then.* At first I wasn't sure what He was talking about, but then I started thinking about Jacob in the Bible and his dream about a ladder leading to heaven. I always have these moments where I can see God working. I thought He meant a linear rung, as in we were going to grow upward, with me at the top and then sixteen tiers or steps down.

Well, a new employee I had recently hired offered a completely different take on what the sixteen rungs meant. He imagined the ladder laying horizontal along the side of a building because you can't grow your team so deep that you become unable to see what's happening. The lightbulb went off.

If I were going to have multiple business lines, I shouldn't go any deeper than probably three to six leaders and staff with each line because I need the agility to pivot if I'm juggling different balls. Horizontal, not vertical. I need the right leaders in the right places with the right teams below and have them all coming together for the greater purpose and their greater good. It is so important to listen to your staff and hear out their ideas. Everyone learns things in their own time by trial and error; we are always learning.

You know how detectives always say there are no coincidences? Well, God has a way of saying the same thing. Months after the ladder dream, my friend Mary was again decorating, this time a larger new office. She had been going around our town taking pictures to print and frame to hang in our office. She had not been present when I discussed my ladder dream. But she later hung a photo of a sixteen-rung ladder *right outside my office*. She had seen the ladder right behind a building in town and thought it would make a good photo. Little did she know it was confirmation that we were on the right path.

You cannot make this stuff up.

God knows that I tend to ask for a sign to confirm I get his message right. Every time I see that photo, I get chills. His words really are clear. We should trust and believe that he wants only good things for us, even when we are presented with barriers set in front of us. We need to trust his words and his love for us and inhale them as we do the air we breathe.

Perhaps the main life lesson I learned in establishing my own company is you must follow your gut and don't listen when people say your innovative ideas are stupid, that they'll never work. I have had so many people try to discourage me. I believe the root of that kind of negativism is the fear of change and a lack of understanding. We need more people supporting and embracing one another. We need to say: *Yes, you can.* So find your cheerleaders and go for it. Be bold. Don't listen to the critics. Let God lead; he won't steer you wrong.

My husband has been a big cheerleader for me. If I come home discouraged, he reminds me giving up is not in our family vocabulary. So I just continue to let God direct. When in doubt take the risk and trust Him. He pushed me off the cliff, and I haven't fallen yet.

~ Chapter 6 ~
Children in Christ

Our actions impact our children. They are watching everything we do. If we cuss, they will cuss. If we smoke, they will likely smoke. If we steal, they will be prone to steal. I implore everyone to please be a good example to our children. Take them to church and let them learn the stories of God.

Train up a child in the way he should go; even when he is old he will not depart from it (Prov. 22:6).

We enrolled our oldest son in a Christian school from kindergarten through fifth grade. It was a private school, and we were blessed enough to get income credits so that he could attend through a grant and church donations. He was able to learn more about the Bible than I likely still know to date. He was able to soak in all the staple stories of Christ. He has become a witness and a leading example through the years, even for me. As of this writing our son is twenty. He is a lot like his father and stays the course. I had no idea what a teen should act like or be. His youth has been completely different from mine, growing up in a rural community in a two-parent household.

In 2014 my husband and I made an intentional decision to move to a small town away from a city environment to protect our marriage and family from the urban hustle and bustle. We wanted better for our children than we had. I didn't want them to grow up in a tough neighborhood or be teased and ridiculed the way I was. I wanted to protect them from all harm. God wants this very thing for us. So, it's important that we make every effort to watch after our children, as Christ does for us.

To be honest I was torn about moving. We had a great house that was close to our church. That was where I got baptized and came to know the Lord, so it held special sentimental and spiritual significance to me. But the move was about our children and a tighter community, so we set about looking for a house outside the city in an area where Andy had grown up.

Our budget was tight, and our options were somewhat limited. Andy kept looking at this one house that had been on the market for six months. It was on five acres. My thought was that it was maybe too big, so I resisted it. But it was in our budget, and we couldn't find anything else. We loved the property, the birds, the land, and the home in the country; it was just really far from family.

We moved, and I was discontent for at least four years. I felt far away from my mom, my family, and what I knew. It was now a twenty- or thirty-minute drive to the grocery store, a forty-minute commute to work, and I was used to being close to everything. The basement kept flooding, and there was a lot of yard work and endless bugs. Our nearest neighbors were a half-acre away, so there was a sense of isolation. I'd think that if we lived in town, then my daughter could go ride a bike with friends who lived closer.

But on the other hand, being in the country *was* beautiful with the trees, birds, and other wildlife. During our first year here, we were blessed to be able to get two horses, Reba, a thoroughbred rescue, gave me a run for my money as a new horse owner, and Tori, being an old Colorado trail horse, was relaxed as ever. I have learned so much from those horses, including how to live in the moment and cherish every second.

The people in the town are farmers, so they have a strong work ethic. And they have the Future Farmers of America, which they don't have in the city. They host things like Drive Your Tractor to School Day, which is always fun. The children enjoy that. My son participated in FFA and learned about agriculture and farming. Again, that's not something he would have gotten in the city.

Then there's an old school mentality in the community of treating others right and living right, looking out for your neighbor. Growing up in the city I was subjected to a lot of drugs, the peer pressure to keep up with my crew—just a wilder environment. I think there's an accountability here that is harder to get in the city because everybody knows everybody. My graduating class in high school had more than five hundred students. Here my sons' had forty. My daughter will graduate with sixty. When the students in school walk down the hallway, they know every face, and they know every family. People know where you live. There are just more guard rails and a genuine sense of community. There are definitely advantages and disadvantages, and I ultimately came to see more pros than cons as I eventually fell in love with it here and find it delightful.

And I was reminded that this had been my dream. A while after we moved, I received a letter I had written shortly before graduating from high school. A teacher had asked us to write a letter to our future selves fifteen years from then. We were to tell our older selves where we wanted to be by the time we reached that age. That teacher then mailed us our letters to us.

I had written: *I want to be married with two children and two horses.* God had put me exactly where I wanted to be. It just took me a while to realize it and appreciate the blessing. My feelings changed, and I began to thrive in this small, quiet country town.

God had wanted to teach me how country life goes. He also wanted to teach me patience. At that time I had to learn quiet patience before I would be able to progress further into his kingdom. One night after working a very long day, I arrived home at about 7:30 p.m. The children had not been fed, and the horses were also due for a meal.

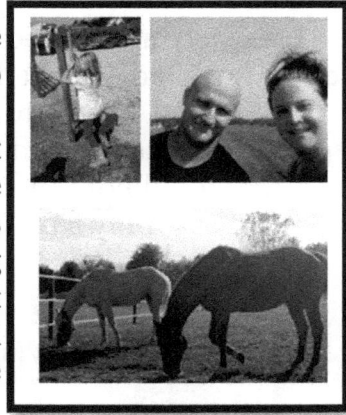

My husband was cooking dinner. My horse, Reba, had been cribbing and chewing up her stall in the run-in barn and had the plywood scuffed up to where she was banging her head on it and getting scratched up. After treating her muzzle and forehead I decided to fix it right then and went to the basement to find a hammer, nail, and piece of wood I could reuse on the barn.

My husband shouted from the back porch, "Just wait and I'll help you."

I thought: *I don't need your help, and I want it done now.* I was so impatient and hurried. I marched off to the barn in the dark to nail the board so I could get to dinner. After about fifteen minutes my husband sent our son out to assist. He couldn't get the nail in either (I later found out that the plywood had been wet, preventing the nail from sinking in).

I began getting very frustrated, so I hit the nail as hard as I could in a very childish way, and it popped back at me and went directly into my left eye. In retrospect it was rather comical because my horse's ears stood straight up as I screamed into the darkness. It was so loud, my neighbor heard me from across the field. I pulled the nail out of my eye and felt immediate burning. I paced back and forth out of embarrassment, trying to tell myself it would be okay.

My son kept saying, "Mom, I think you need to go to the hospital."

I resisted, mostly because I didn't want to go inside and face my husband, who had been *right;* I should have waited.

In the end I went to the hospital. I had an eye globe rupture. The doctors said I should have lost my eye and was lucky that it did not cause permanent blindness. Now I just wear glasses for my left eye.

Family solidarity. My father and kids supporting me by wearing a matching eyepatch

But it was not luck that the nail hit exactly where it did. It was a real miracle. It was God. How else is it that 99 percent of people who get a nail in their eye go blind or lose it, and I didn't? A hair lower and I would have been blind; a hair higher I would have lost my eye. I had been impatient all my life. Bossy, independent, and not needing anything from anybody. Well, Lord, I learned my lesson. Slow down and let people help. Stop being so hasty. It took this injury to teach me, and God knew exactly what I needed.

Now I often wonder where I would be if my husband had not asked me to move to a small country town. But for as good as the move turned out to be for me, I believe the move was even better for our children. I'm very impressed by them.

Our son Brydon was baptized during our time here and felt a calling to come to know the Lord. It was very touching among everything that was happening. He's the responsible one who makes sure that the keys are taken and that nobody's drinking and driving. He's always been in line, even if his friends take too far.

Our daughter Gabby has been baptized, has a Bible she highlights verses in, and is learning more every day. I am so thankful she shows an interest, and we can encourage each other to read. Everyone at her school knows she's a Christian. She's an acolyte at our church and continues to grow in her faith. What a beautiful soul she has.

Kinnedy, my daughter from another mother, sings at her church and is actively involved. She chose a Christian college and is deeply rooted in her faith. It's been a blessing to see her blossom.

I think they all have a lot more wits about them than I did at that age; they just walk the right line. Maybe that's because my husband is firm and more involved, and we guard them more. I did not have the shelter and guidance that they've had at all. My mother didn't really set curfews, and staying out late was normalized. She did not tighten up the reins as much as I felt she could have, so all her children touched the fire more times than they should have. There are people who have to touch the fire to learn their own lesson; that was me. And then there are people who go *I was told not to touch the fire, so I'm not going to touch it.* That's my children.

While I believe I offer guardrails to my children, I'm not really a disciplinarian. I'm not Ms. Tough Guy. I give that to my husband because my mom was hyper-critical at times, and I worry about the apple not falling far enough from the tree. To this day I am prone to criticizing myself, even if it's just over something harmlessly stupid. I wanted to make sure I severed myself from that behavior as part of my soul cleansing too. I need to start a new generational pattern for my children and didn't want to lead with criticism.

Our time here on earth can reflect how we want to spend eternity. Heaven on earth can be real when we believe and do what God is guiding us to do. By our example we help guide our children in his light and glory as well.

• Our children Kinnedy, Brydon, and Gabby through the years.

~ Chapter 7 ~
Forgive Others—and Yourself

A round 2018 my pastor asked everyone one Sunday: *Is all well with your soul?* The impact of that question almost left me breathless because I realized all was very *not* well with my soul. It wasn't well with friends, past acquaintances, my family, or myself. I felt a calling to work on myself to cleanse past hurts and trauma, to cleanse my soul. That is how this book began and the journey until now. I made a mental list of the things and relationships I wanted to work on. Top of that list was forgiving myself.

My teenage years and the sins of my youth have troubled me all my adult life. I had written a letter when I was a teen about my troubles and sins during that time. I had saved it in a box all these years, turning back to it to recount the mistakes I made whenever it would call.

I would open that box and read the letter and mourn. It was the worst feeling of deep regret. Shortly after my baptism, the letter called to me while cleaning out my closet. I thought: *I don't want my children to see this. This is between God and me. This is my sin, and I no longer need to stand in sin and depression.* So I burned the letter and forgave myself for my sins. The quiet country home and outside firepit became my space to heal. I needed this place. I cried and prayed and asked for God's forgiveness.

It was still there to some degree, but that was the first step in my soul-cleansing journey. I don't worry about judgment anymore. God is my healer and protector.

Pasts are important. We need to know where we came from to know where we are headed. We need to look at our family traits and dynamics—what worked and what didn't? Then pause and reflect to see what we should or could learn from those moments.

Blessed are the pure in heart; for they shall see God (Matthew 5:8).

There was a marketing vendor my company worked with for a while, and when our relationship was coming to a close, he said we should stay in touch and gave me some advice: *You don't have to burn down the whole bridge when you close a relationship.* I reflected on this statement a lot because it hit home. Unintentionally and unknowingly, in past relationships when I got honked off at somebody, I'd blow up and cut whoever it was off, even if just harboring hurt in my head. But he reminded me that you don't have to do that, personally or professionally. You can walk away and regroup.

That sage bit of advice fit right in with getting my soul right. I want to live on this earth in peace and joy and have camaraderie with people I deal with on a day-to-day basis; I don't want any brewing animosity or bitterness. So now I try very hard to be the *don't burn the bridge* kind of person; I don't ever want to harm a relationship.

But it wasn't always that way. And back when the pastor asked his question, there were people in my life I felt I had harmed. So I took personal responsibility through self-assessment, something I think we have to do as humans. Part of that process of deep healing was journaling, which allowed me to get a more profound awareness of myself and where I was in life and receive deeper inspiration from the spirit, who had led and guided me throughout my life, even when I wasn't aware of it.

After I had begun the process of self-forgiveness, I started getting my soul right with others. As an example say I had told someone in high school that I disliked them. If that's still there and it's a trigger or it's bringing up feelings that shouldn't have been, that's what my goal was on this journey to get right. Mending and patching are now the standard. I think we all tend to relive moments; I know I do—*I shouldn't have said that. I should have done this better.* But most of the work involved current relationships, not only people I used to know when I was younger.

With a lot of prayer, I started calling people to tell them I was sorry for whatever had transpired. Whether it was my fault or not didn't matter; it was important to get my soul right. That included my mother.

As I alluded to before, our time working together was very hard for me. Every conversation felt *too* personal. I pushed myself harder and harder every day, yet it never seemed to be enough. We did family mentoring with a business coach. It helped a bit to release the feelings we had, but it did not help me in the business. I was working at my mother's dream. God started to call me to my own interests. I needed to find my own dream and find delight in my work.

I believe we should enjoy our work and our calling, asking God to help us get there. We should be in places and careers that we truly enjoy and feel that we are making a difference. We need to be fed spiritually in each moment.

I decided to leave the family business and trusted God had bigger plans for me. I had gone as far as I could there and needed to have my mother, just be my mom again. God does not want us completely absorbed with work. Yes, we must work, but it should be done in joy.

Looking back now, several years after leaving the family business, I know it was the best professional decision I ever made. I have been following God into deeper relationships. He wants us to be entrepreneurs in life, to take bountiful leaps of faith. Every day I do exactly what he tells me to do although I do sometimes question to make sure I heard him clearly. I jumped into the deep end with only him as my raft.

I am blessed by my mother and the way that she molded me. Our relationship has not always been easy, but we are good friends. I love her immensely. She will always have that special place in my heart as my mentor and friend. Even though we are busy with life, children, and work, we are still able to chat on the phone or have lunch together.

As time passed, I found myself moving on to others in my life, in particular the lost sheep, the one person I have never mended with. In fact, I had to part ways. I just cannot be around them. Sometimes you must accept that others have to deal with traumas and whatever else they're harboring on their own—you absolutely cannot take that on. You need a protective bubble, so you don't get sucked in.

I told this familial lost sheep that I was sorry for the discord between us. But they were not willing to meet me even a fraction of the way. They have so much drama in their life that causes them and others so much harm. I finally understood I could not fix that. I can fix myself, but I can't fix others, especially if they don't want to mend the relationship, if they don't want help getting their soul right. It's a painful realization but an important one.

You can't be a spiritual enabler. You need to set that idea down or else it will inevitably harm you and your soul. You can't fall back into the habit of thinking it's your fault they have a troubled life. *What have I done wrong? How can I change to reach them?* I wish this person the best and pray for them all the time, but I can't fix them.

I don't want to sound melodramatic, but I know many people who have watched friends and family battle addiction, and the hold substance abuse can have on a person can be almost demonic because it's like they literally become someone other than the person you used to know. People often turn to drugs, alcohol, and bad choices because it numbs their pain or acts as self-medication for depression and other emotional issues. This is my prayer for all who suffer:

> *Therefore, rid yourselves of all malice and all deceit, hypocrisy, envy, and slander of every kind. Like newborn babies, crave pure spiritual milk, so that by it you may grow up in your salvation, now that you have tasted that the Lord is good.*

> *The Living Stone and a Chosen People*

> *As you come to him, the living Stone—rejected by humans but chosen by God and precious to him— you also, like living stones, are being built into a spiritual house to be a holy priesthood, offering spiritual sacrifices acceptable to God through Jesus Christ. For in scripture it says:*

> *"See, I lay a stone in Zion, a chosen and precious cornerstone, and the one who trusts in him will never be put to shame."*

> *Now to you who believe, this stone is precious. But to those who do not believe,*

> *"The stone the builders rejected has become the cornerstone," and, "A stone that causes people to stumble and a rock that makes them fall."*

> *They stumble because they disobey the message— which is also what they were destined for.*

> *But you are a chosen people, a royal priesthood, a holy nation, God's special possession, that you may declare the praises of him who called you out of darkness into his wonderful light. Once you*

were not a people, but now you are the people of God; once you had not received mercy, but now you have received mercy (1 Peter 2–10).

When people do not have the full armor of God, the devil gets in their ear and tells them they're not good enough. I've been there. But friends you *are* good enough. All you have to do is ask for help to change; you must want to change and be diligent. God wants to see that in your heart. Redemption is here; you only have to let him in.

To all that don't know him: I pray you find your way in Christ. Your life will change for the better. The ultimate message is to get well with your soul and experience joy on earth, not allowing any hurt or harm to penetrate your well-being. And that's a hard thing to do. Working through my past hurts and harms left me feeling so much better, so much lighter.

But let's be clear: it's not always an easy conversation. In my case, with one notable exception, I think most people were receptive, but even then, not everyone accepts amends necessarily in the way you'd hoped. Continually work through that, pray and process. When you get the soul cleansed, it bestows a peace that leaves you feeling stronger both physically and mentally as well as spiritually. It's so impactful.

~ Chapter 8 ~

Earthly and Heavenly Fathers

I believe God puts people in our life to help fill voids and be angels of direction and encouragement. When I was little, another friend's dad, Larry, was a very sweet role model. One day we were riding our bikes, and I got stung by a bee. It hurt so badly, and I was an utter mess, crying hysterically over the teeniest little sting. Larry raced over, scooped me up, and took me inside where his wife, Tina, put a baking soda-water mix on it. It was the first time I remember being picked up and carried by a man. My father left when I was very young, so I had no memories of him holding me or that love as a child. I remember looking into Larry's kind eyes and seeing his great reassuring smile and true concern. I thought *This is what it's like to have a dad.*

At that point I didn't know what it was like to have a father. My mom dated a bit, but that wasn't important to her. She waited until we were out of high school to remarry. Now, I have a terrific stepdad. He has been a shining example of encouragement and support. I have been very blessed to have him in my life and to have a relationship with my father as an adult.

But growing up with a father impacts your life in so many subtle ways. For example, because I did not grow up with a stern male voice, I honestly think men are yelling at me every time they get a little upset about something. Our tone is so important. Sure, there are times when we express disappointment or annoyance—if it's followed by a place of love. Many people take anger and frustration too far.

Because I had grown up without a father, I also had no idea what family looked like. I had no idea what a successful marriage looked like. As an adult I yearned to know my father. After high school I reached out and started calling my dad to reconnect and establish a relationship. We both have apologized.

Now that my dad and I have found each other in my adulthood, having him in my life is so very important, and I just love him dearly. I wished he lived closer, but his home is in Oklahoma. His family is there, and he occupies the generational land of his father. But we find excuses to see each other and make a diligent effort to check in with each other. We talk almost once a week, and I love the conversations we have together. Through them I've come to see that my father is an awesome man of God. We find delight in talking about the Lord. He is such a humble, godly man. He admits his faults and asks for forgiveness.

I'm not sure my father has forgiven himself for leaving, but God forgives! I wish he would see that. And I have forgiven him. The ways of this world are shallow, but the heavens call us to love and compassion. It has been very nice to build a relationship with my father. Hopefully, if he reads this, he'll know that I love him so very much, and he is absolutely a great father!

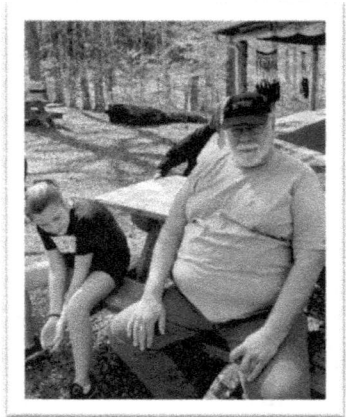

MY FATHER, DON AND MY DAUGHTER, GABBY IN 2019.

~ Chapter 9 ~
Marriage

Next on the journey to get my soul right was my relationship with my husband. I waited until everything else in my soul had been worked out to confront this. Anyone who has been married knows how complex such a union is.

At that point we had been together nearly twenty years. More than half my life. What makes marriage so hard is that people constantly evolve, so how do you navigate that? We had struggled, which often ended in arguments, sometimes in front of our children. I had been praying for God to show me a way to break through what seemed to be an insurmountable compatibility issue.

We would argue but never really get to the heart of what was not working. One day I got so frustrated I was finally able to pinpoint to myself what I was missing.

I am done, I thought. *I am done arguing and fighting for no reason. No more anger. I want to be friends; I want to laugh again. I WANT TO DANCE.*

I wrote a long letter to my husband outlining that very moment. The next day I was at a small business conference, manning a booth with a coworker and talking to prospective clients. I took the first break and left to grab a snack. When I got back, as my coworker was walking away to take their lunch break, a man came up. Perfect timing so we could talk openly. Even though we were in the middle of this conference, it felt like just us. I locked into his eyes as a dear brother in Christ as he approached my booth. On his angelic white shirt was a fire logo above the business name Reclaiming Marriages. My heart dropped because just the night before, my husband and I had this huge conversation about how we could improve our marriage.

He said, "You look like you need to talk," in the most heart-catching way.

There's no doubt in my mind that he was an angel sent by God. This man couldn't have any knowledge of the argument between my husband and me the night before. He met me at my weakest point. It took all I had not to burst into tears and break down at my booth. I pretended like nothing was wrong to hold it together for the conference and kept it all business, but we did exchange business cards.

That night I went home and gave the card to my husband, telling him that God wanted our marriage to succeed and had sent this man to us. How amazing it was. A resource and help. I asked my husband to call this man if he wanted to work on our marriage.

This marriage mission to reclaim our marriage felt right in my heart. It was a feeling of warmth, and I knew God had his hand on this. The company is led by a married man and woman in Westerville, Ohio, who have their own story—another couple who had walked this path before. They became like a breath of fresh air to us. God had pulled them up out of the fire, and now he wanted to save our marriage.

We met with the man for more than six months, nearly twenty sessions. We even increased the number of sessions to ensure we would be able to get it all in. I cried during every session, and I had no idea how much I had been through. How much I had hurt him, talked badly to him—and vice versa. Suddenly, my attitude and the way I approached the situation was on me. The roles reversed. It was clear. Love is a totally *unselfish* emotion. When we love we receive love. We need to put God in the center of our marriage, pray together, and submit to one another. Let your husband really lead. It's a friendship.

I wanted more than anything for my children to witness how to have a healthy, loving marriage. It's now that time. We are a living testimony of once having had a bad marriage filled with contempt, anger, mistrust, and arguing to a blossoming friendship every day.

My husband is the kindest person and does anything to make me happy. He brews me coffee in the mornings and helps with my laundry when I must work. I'm not saying times are never rough, and we do get on each other's nerves at times, but it is much better now than ever. We are friends again. We have healed from generational cycles and demonic influences. With God's help and the help of Reclaiming Marriages, our marriage was saved. He used this as a branch to heaven. We would not be here without them. Having a safe zone and teaching about what love really looks like is so important. The visionary goal I have and yearn for is to be the last ones standing at a wedding when they call for the longest-running marriage—at the age of eighty!

If you are at odds with anyone in your family—siblings, parents, spouse, children—I strongly recommend you make amends. Jesus wants us to love one another. God wants us to live fully in the love and abounding glory he has for us. When we love our family and find ways to put smiles on their faces, we smile with them. When we heal old wounds and reach out to one another, we bridge the gap from the unknown to the known; we make things right with our souls.

Similarly to finding moments of joy, I encourage you to unravel the mysteries. The moments in which you were not your best self. I want to encourage you to remember your past, as this is where sometimes there are things that need to be healed. Uncovering your purposes and depths is often difficult, especially if there is trauma. If needed, seek professional counseling in addition to talking with the Lord.

As hard as it is, you need to unpack and acknowledge situations that you didn't like, things you did that you wished that you could undo. Bringing these things to light—whatever they may be—brings us closer to detoxifying your soul and closer to being born-again and into a deeper relationship with God.

It took four years, but I can finally say that all is indeed right with my soul. I am happy, set free. Sure, every day has its challenges, but I am like a small child on the pillows and clouds of heaven. My Lord and savior is near, and nothing will stand against me again! He has lifted me from the depths of despair. I am blessed.

I am still troubled by certain moments and pray for them. I am still tempted, but I immediately ask God for forgiveness. Every ungodly thought is immediately replaced and turned back to God. We need to be in constant communion with him. And there is certainly more that I want to ask God to help me build upon. But my sin and self-hatred are both gone.

~ Chapter 10 ~
Signs of Confirmation

I don't know if it's because I came to God and the Bible later in life or what, but as I mentioned earlier, I need to have visual signs as affirmation and confirmation. Well, ask God for a sign of confirmation, and he will provide one.

There's an interesting spiritual sidenote about my paternal grandmother, Grandma Pat. Numbers have great significance in the Bible, and she was born and passed away on the same day: July 11. I believe her life was full of both good and bad, and she landed in the hands of her father. While searching scripture regarding 711 verses, I found Matthew 7:11, and it resonated with me.

> *If ye then, being evil, know how to give good gifts unto your children, how much more shall your Father which is in heaven give good things to them that ask him?*

The Lord wants us to find treasures here on earth and to know that we can ask for anything. He will help to provide it. God gives us signs and wonders all over the place. We should listen and trust that small still voice, planting our feet firmly in him and his word. He is our foundation, and he will give us a white stone with a new name. He will find ways to connect with us; animals, birds, visions, and thoughts are all from him. If we cannot hear him, perhaps there are things we need to rid of in our minds and souls first. Knowing God is about you being 100 percent pure to hear his voice, then doing the calling he has placed you on the earth to do.

Is he asking us to do something first? Is he asking us to forgive or tell someone something? I had to clear every burden from my shoulders, every negative thought. Everything he tells us to do—or not to do—we must follow. It has taken me years to hear him clearly. And now when I don't, I know that I must study more of his scriptures and continue to learn. I am so thankful that I can open my Bible to exactly where and what he wants me to learn.

Numbers especially speak to me, specifically 333, 7, 33, 111, and 13. My daughter loves 222, and maybe you can relate to having a sign as confirmation that God is near. When I am low and feel discouraged, I see him at that moment. I can be driving and see a license plate or sign that directs me to a certain Bible passage. I pull over, read it, and it is usually spot on. If you look for him, he will show you; for me it can be in four-leaf clovers, eagles, and bluebirds.

> *Afterward he appeared unto the eleven as they sat at meat and upbraided them with their unbelief and hardness of heart, because they believed not them which had seen him after he was risen.*
>
> *And he said unto them, Go ye into all the world, and preach the gospel to every creature.*
>
> *He that believeth and is baptized shall be saved; but he that believeth not shall be damned.*
>
> *And these signs shall follow them that believe; In my name shall they cast out devils; they shall speak with new tongues.*
>
> *They shall take up serpents; and if they drink any deadly thing, it shall not hurt them; they shall lay hands on the sick, and they shall recover.*
>
> *So then after the Lord had spoken unto them, he was received up into heaven, and sat on the right hand of God.*

And they went forth, and preached everywhere, the Lord working with them, and confirming the word with signs following. Amen (Mark 16:14–20).

If you look for him, he will show you ...

Captions left to right from top: We took my son to do a college visit in Florida and stayed a long weekend at the Wyndham resort. The address was 333. • My daughter sent this to me on Instagram when she saw the number of likes as 333. • On the phone with a coworker and discussing business in IL airport. As we were talking, a wheelchair came up and was parked right in front of me with 333 on the back. • A truck on the road. • California conference led to was at 333 O Farrell St. • Went in for my daughter's parent teacher conference and found Math 333 written on the board. • File size on important document was 333. • Cars on the road

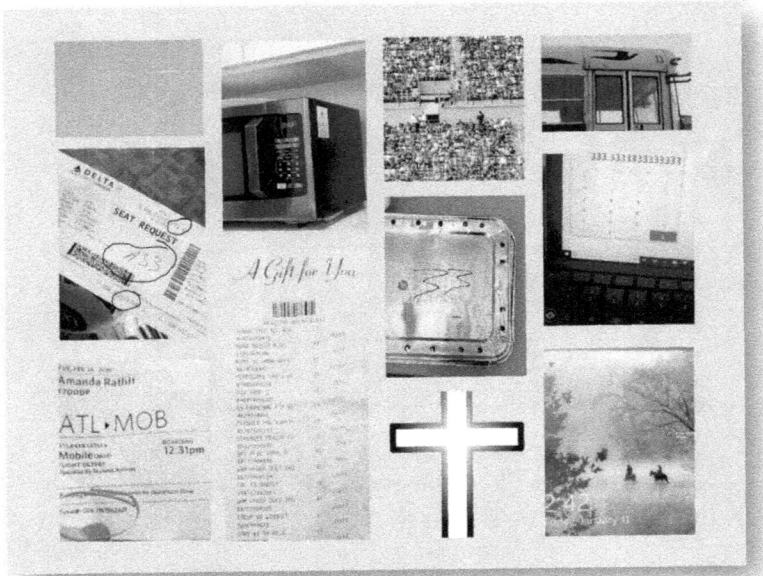

Left to right from top left: On vacation while relaxing on sofa, a cross was formed by two airplanes. • Making my lunch one day, I saw two microwaves with 33 seconds on them. • I went to a NASCAR race with my husband and after sitting down I was directly in front of section 333. • My daughter's school bus number. • My business flight was delayed but I was not discouraged because my gate was A33, and 777 and 333 were in my reference numbers. • I ordered Buffalo Wild Wings for the team, the order number was 33. • The first calculation of costs for a project I was under pressure for. • The ticket for my first trip back to Mobile, Alabama, after thirty-plus years showed my birthday 6/21—twice! • Buying wedding gifts for an old coworker and 333 marked the entire receipt as a blessing to her. • My friend Ginny sent me this picture of us riding on Jan 11 (111), and God spoke to me that she was my friend.

And sometimes the message can also be a warning. I was on a business call with someone I had been warned about and was not feeling good about how the conversation was going. Each time the person spoke, a truck with a snake logo would pull in front of me. [[snake]] When he stopped speaking, it would go behind as we were backlogged in traffic. It was a sign to be on guard and watch myself. God will lead you if you let him.

Maybe it's an algorithm in AI sending me 333 on my phone, but how can this be while I am traveling down the freeway and see them exactly at the moment I need to? Here is perfect proof: I was traveling from Columbus to Cincinnati for a conference early one morning. Something caused me to stop at a McDonald's for coffee. I could have driven another twenty miles or five or ten instead of stopping at this one. I could have used the drive-through, but I chose to go in. I could have been ten minutes earlier or later. But I was in the right place at the right time be customer number 333. I watched as the printed ticket for the customer in front of me was 332. One order off, I would not have had that happen! Only God can do that.

Chapter 11

Do Not Cry

This was another big lesson I had to learn. I have been a crybaby all my life. No lie. I would cry when I didn't get my way, cry when I was hangry, cry at movies, and cry when someone said something mean to me. I literally cried almost every day. I believe it was all the mush I had inside.

God wanted me to learn not to cry.

I was given the biggest job I had ever had in my life—a small business with a big task—a client who wanted more but didn't want to pay for it or take the time to communicate or plan. It was challenging, tiring, and scary, and I wanted to literally give up after the client called and chewed me out. I have never been yelled at so hard in my life. I kept trying to explain the difficulties that we were having—which were all valid—but they didn't want excuses. We couldn't have a reason to fail, so I stopped with the excuses. This had been months and months of work, and both parties were tired.

At the end of his stern vent, I simply said, "Okay, I understand, sir. I will fix it."

He thanked me, and we ended the call. I had two minutes to decide whether I was going to cry or go to my next meeting and fix it. I had no time.

I teared up, glanced to the heavens, and said, "Okay, Lord, help me get through this."

And since that day I stopped crying. I realized that everyone makes mistakes and has challenges and problems to overcome. Sure, I am sad and have trying moments, but I'm no longer going to cry about it. I'm honestly thankful now for that man who yelled so hard at me that day. He gave me the aptitude and spirit to resolve the issues. This was business.

It's the same way with God; he has to get angry and ask you to change. He will keep putting barriers, bad days, accidents, and obstacles in your path to learn what you need to learn. Until you learn from it, you will never move on to the next item to make you complete.

Life is literally a test. He wants us to walk on the clouds in heaven. Life should be like floating. If it's not, I challenge you to seek God's wisdom and clarity in every moment of your life. All it takes is faith and belief that he will fulfill his mission for you. All things work together for his good.

~ Chapter 12 ~

Give Hilariously

God loves a cheerful giver.
~2 Corinthians 9:7

I was led to hire a well-known consultant in our industry to help with my company years ago. He has helped to guide and lead us, and I consider him a brother. I believe that he was brought into my life as a protector. His father was a Baptist preacher and knew much about the Bible. We often bounce ideas off each other and try to analyze what God is saying in our lives.

While working with this consultant, I learned so much about tithing and how we should always seek opportunities to give unto others. He sent me a book about tithing and possessions after I was struggling with some small successes in making revenue and how to give back. I'd been very frugal and wanted to help others more than purchase earthly things. This book talks about how you should not store possessions on earth. It is so true! This is not our money. It is given to us by God. We must consult him with every purchase and tithe. God calls us to give.

The story of the widow's mites, which is told in the gospels of Mark and Luke, was an interesting revelation to me as a newfound Christian. In the story, *mites* refer to a coin comparable to our penny.

One day Jesus was sitting with his disciples near the temple treasury, watching the wealthy faithful giving large sums of money. Then a widow walked up and put two mites into the offering receptacle. Jesus pointed her out to his disciples.

Truly I tell you, this poor widow has put more into the treasury than all the others. They all gave out of their wealth; but she, out of her poverty, put in everything, all she had to live on (Mark 12:43–44).

There are several things the story tells us. First, God values the quality of giving, not quantity. Second, God appreciates true sacrifice. Last, God wants us to give in faith. And to know that he will see to our needs, so even if the widow gave the last of her money, God made sure she was provided for.

So give all you have left and help the poor.

Chapter 13

Dreams and Visions from Above

I had the opportunity to go to New York with some girlfriends to relax a bit after eighteen months of nonstop work. We got massages, and as I lay there I had a peaceful vision. I was on this beautiful mountain looking out at pine hills, radiant purple and orange against a darkening sky. I felt the gentle wind on my face and was at complete rest.

The air smelled so lovely, and all of a sudden I heard God's voice. *You're on top of the mountain.*

I asked: *What Lord?*

He said: *Your climb is over. You made it. It won't be any harder than this.*

I couldn't believe it, but it was another profound moment with my heavenly father. I ran up to the hotel room and called my husband to check in. He was in Pennsylvania that weekend, visiting a college with our son, and I shared the vision and how terrific and full of joy I was that the Lord had spoken to me.

Sometimes we just need to pause, rest, and seek his word. He will speak in different ways, and it is never the same for everyone.

Here are some additional samples of how he talked with me and walked with me.

Vision of the Liberty Bell and Being on a Mountaintop

God gave me a vision showing how to build a software system with team design. I felt like he was giving me the blueprints for my life at every intersection. I trust that the Lord is working for my good and at his timing and his will. I am just his servant, following his direction.

Shell Napkin

After my dream about being reborn, I went to Sunday school for a lesson on God wiping our sins away. The teacher's wife had gone out to buy napkins to demonstrate how easily we can be cleaned and dried with God's love. Guess what the napkins had on them?

Shells. And not just any shells. The exact shells that I saw in my dream. (My pastor told me that shells symbolize rebirth and a new chance.) The teacher could have bought any other kind of napkins, but no, God guided her to get the shell napkins. It's amazing how he finds ways to speak to us. Listen to him. These small ways of communicating with us are kisses from heaven to show us we are exactly where we are supposed to be.

God Told Me to Hire a Specific Software Developer

I had been debating about it for a while. I was taking a walk in the harbor, asking God what to do.

He said very clearly: *I've told you what to do*, telling me again the name very clearly.

As I walked along still waiting for a sign and not seeing anything that clearly identified the name—remember, I look for confirmation in visual signs—I decided to head back to the room to get ready for the day.

On the way back I saw a homeless man pacing around the park, looking through trash cans, under benches, etc., for food or money. He trotted everywhere at a fast pace. God told me to take him to breakfast.

I was like: *Lord, I don't know where to take him. I am not from here. What if he harms me?*

Besides that, my husband is a police officer and warned me not to take risks, especially in unknown places.

God said again: *Just take him to breakfast. He needs to see me, and I will protect you.*

He pushed me again. I kept debating and fighting back on why I couldn't.

"He is getting too far, Lord; he's on the other side of the harbor now."

As soon as I said it, he told me to ask the jogger running by to pass the message that I wanted to take the homeless man to breakfast and come back.

"I can't, Lord; I just can't."

He urged me again. *This man needs me; find another way.*

Just then a police officer in a golf cart rolled by.

There you go, said God. *Ask the policeman to take you over there if you don't feel safe. Tell him you need to deliver a message.*

I said, "No, Lord, I can't do it. I don't even have makeup on."

Okay, I know—stupid excuse. The golf cart drove off. I'd waited too long.

The man was miles away, and I could barely see him. I gave up. Walking away discouraged, I rounded a corner of three beautiful trees, and the wind raged through the trees and almost blew me off my feet. Three large gusts out of nowhere. There had been absolutely no wind that morning until then.

God pushed me back. *I said go ask the man to breakfast!*

"Okay, okay, okay, Lord. I will find a way."

I headed back to the harbor, but the man was gone. I missed my chance.

Then God said: *I told you, if you don't hire this software developer I asked you to, it will be too late. You must do what I say when I say it, or your chance will disappear.*

I was in awe. God had given me the answer all within this one-hour walk around the harbor praying. I hired the software developer that day, and they are amazing. As confirmation I found out right after hiring them that one of their best teammates was planning to move out of the country for a professorship thirty days later. We would need him to design the best tool before he left.

Okay, lesson learned. Had I not secured him at that moment, I would have lost my chance. Trust your gut and listen to the instructions.

~ Chapter 14 ~
Persevere and He Shall Provide

I read a book called *Draw the Circle: The 40-Day Prayer Challenge*, which is about developing a more impactful prayer life by praying on those things that are important to you and that you want to circle in your life so it will grow and flourish. Two parts of that book stuck out to me. The first is a section that talks about how the birds will sing and the delight of the land and the flowers they are talking about.

"Talk to the birds, and they'll talk back to you."

The point is God created these birds for you to enjoy and listen to. You don't have to tell other people everything; talk to the birds, and they'll talk back. So of course I found myself one morning on my porch talking to a robin that was sitting on the fence. This robin frequents that spot, and I had seen it there before, waiting for me for weeks. I opened up. And I tell you it sat there and listened the whole time until I was done.

I'm sure if anybody had walked by and seen me talking to a bird, they would probably think I was nuts. I mean, although I wasn't speaking aloud, it was admittedly weird. But I didn't care; I was loving every moment. I was talking to this robin. And I felt much lighter and more connected to God afterward.

As I continued with this book, drawing circles about important prayers needed that needed answering in my life. One story that struck me talked about agricultural scientist George Washington Carver, who would get up at 4:00 a.m. to pray each and every morning for direction and clarity. Carver studied crop-rotation methods in the United States, teaching Southern farmers how to rotate soil-depleting crops like cotton with soil-enriching crops like peanuts, sweet potatoes, and peas. However, while it helped assure bumper crops of cotton, it also resulted in a surplus of peanuts.

Carver prayed on the problem and then went to work finding alternative uses for peanuts. He ended up developing more than three hundred products from peanuts, everything from cooking oil to cosmetics. (Contrary to popular belief, he did not invent peanut butter. John Harvey Kellogg filed a patent for peanut butter in 1895.) But the point is that Carver prayed, persisted in working for a solution, and God provided him with answers and multiplied it abundantly.

I can relate. I love my line of work, and he is providing the stepping stones for me to work on what I love. I have needed help, and every day he provides me with new directions and answers to prayers—never more so than during and after the pandemic.

We saw so many small businesses completely shut down in the last two years, and I came close to closing my business. In 2020 I had to lay off many of my great team members and work family, which was horrible. I have a women-owned small, disadvantaged business that is certified by the Women's Business Enterprise National Council, but government and commercial clients stopped soliciting bids. Everything stalled, and we did not see sources of work.

I was so invested in the business, and it seemed like I spent two years pursuing potential clients, trying to convince larger companies to work with me. It was constant pushing and worrying; I almost burned out my adrenal glands. I also had some medical stuff happening and surgeries I needed to have. I was just physically and emotionally spent. I was not seeing a way to succeed, and at the end of 2021, I wanted to collapse. We have a great business with much to offer, but everything had dried up.

I thought: *I'm done; I can't do this anymore. I have tried and tried and tried. There are no sales. I've made every phone call known to man. I've begged and pleaded. I've borrowed. I literally want to close.*

But my husband wouldn't let me give up out of frustration. He told me: *You've worked too hard; don't give up now. Hang in there a little bit longer.* So I kept going and kept praying. And slowly but surely these relationships I'd been working on for years finally started coming to together.

I got a call from one of the partners on it, and they said, "Amanda, we've called eight other businesses, and you're the only one that has healthcare and technology, and we need you on this."

Between that and my husband's encouragement, I agreed to hang on a little bit longer. We did our oral presentations in March and won it in June. It's a five-year contract, which provides longer-term stability for my team and brings jobs to the community. There were four other companies that bid, and we were the only one that communicated and exhibited high confidence. Even more amazing is that we were the highest priced, but they picked us anyway because of our proprietary technology; they wanted emerging innovation.

So that was a good day with God's promise confirmed, and I must have thought, *Oh, thank you, Lord,* a hundred times. In June 2022 we won our first big software as a service contract—finally. The blessing and fruits of our labor. It was a bid we had submitted two years earlier. It sat and sat and sat for so long that I had bowed out of it previously, but it circled back to me. Since then we have been able to hire ten more people. I've got my team—who are completely devoted—humming again and going back after it. Because my company has such unique and diverse capabilities, it does give us an advantage in the marketplace over our competitors. And we are centrally located so it's easy to span our reach into other states nationally. Now that people are getting together in person again, we've picked up, and we finally have the business stabilized.

The bid we won couldn't be more important on a human level. We get to work with a unique and sensitive project. It's truly a blessing, and words can't describe how honored we are to get this opportunity. It's amazing.

And the blessings keep coming. The local Procurement Technical Assistance Centers office that helps women-owned small businesses told me they want to do a success story on how ARC Healthcare and ARC's Family of Companies came out of the horrible COVID period, with layoffs and limited opportunities, to regain our footing—and then some. So it's all exciting and really remarkable how with perseverance, hope, and encouragement we have succeeded.

My prayers were truly answered by this contract. It allowed me to keep the staff that we've trained and developed and continue to grow our company family, our team members, and our culture, and then pay down some of the debt that we accrued during COVID. And continue to add jobs.

We also got a $25,000 grant from an organization called JobsOhio, which we will use to establish a small hub office that will house our computers and other IT equipment. With this we can continue to operate remotely and ship computers to people where they live. We plan to continue growing to scale with call center and other business process outsourcing. In a lot of states, they have different set-asides and funding assistance and grants for small businesses. I am so proud of where we are going and what we have become. It's a big win for us to showcase our technology, our team, and our skill sets. All thanks to holding onto the dream and promise God has for our lives.

It's such a breath of fresh air that wouldn't have happened without prayer, persistence, and God providing.

Chapter 15

Your Moment Is Now

God wants us to have heaven on earth. He is waiting and hoping for us to make earth heaven. This very moment is our test to take up the cross and stand by him. To speak up for him. To testify and share. To keep his spirit alive and keep his name on our tongue. Each morning the sun rises and falls to glorious light. Each day we have a chance to make a difference. No matter your circumstances, sisters and brothers, please take it to God, and he will help.

We are in a world where at times, we do not love one another, which is the very thing we were created to do. Love. Honor. Respect. Listen to one another. It is simple, and yet we make it hard. I believe there are still lessons to learn about embracing love over success. Family over career. Compassion over impressions.

When I fell off that golden copper fountain in my dream of being reborn, I heard my family and others laughing at me, but not in a bad way. It was filled with a childlike spirit and felt peaceful. Do you remember the last time you fell, someone laughed, and you felt embarrassed? It didn't feel like that; it was pleasant, harmlessly glee-filled.

Please consider how your family comes together—or doesn't. How might you rectify that relationship? How might you pray for change or pray for them? How might you right the wrong? Do you need to forgive someone, or do you need to apologize? Think about who you might be at odds with, and then fix it as Jesus would. Walk in his spirit. It will release so you may abound in him.

I often wonder what meeting God our father will be like. Will we get to sit on his lap? Will we get to hug him with tears streaming down our faces? Will we drop to our knees and bow at his feet? What do you imagine you will do when you meet your father, the creator? I certainly do not want to dirty his white robe. When I think of hugging him now, even though I have been forgiven, I feel spiritually unclean, not as worthy as I would like to feel. So, I ask myself: *Will I ever feel clean enough to touch or talk with God?* But what I then realize is that he's not going to care. He is the maker. He wants the best for us and loves us no matter what. There is no judgment. No condemnation.

As you read this, think about what God did for you. The son of God died so you can choose wrong or right, up or down, evil or good. You have free will and to do wrong is wrong. Right is right, but oftentimes we choose wrong and wicked. Temptation overtakes us. We curse, lie, steal, and commit sins against our families and others. And I say *we* because no one is blameless.

> *How can you think of saying, 'Friend, let me help you get rid of that speck in your eye,' when you can't see past the log in your own eye? Hypocrite! First get rid of the log in your own eye; then you will see well enough to deal with the speck in your friend's eye .*

I have taken the log out of my own eye so I can cry out to you, my friends: please turn toward Christ. He wants nothing more than to fill you with his overwhelming and endless love. We all have specks, imperfections, and battles; we are called to hold each other accountable in this life.

I continue to have unbelievable testimonies of God's works on my life. But I will end here with a simple observation: *your story with God never ends.* There is always a new place, a level higher, another awesome miracle. You must cherish them and look for him daily. His signs are everywhere. We must continue to be friends, advocates to and for one another, and share the good news. People learn by hearing and trusting, and we are called to plant the seed of the spirit.

You need to choose your path: Good or bad? Light or dark? Up or down? You only get one shot and your moment is now. Try my friends to live and see the blessings. Live in righteousness and be kind to one another.

Prayer of Salvation: Our First Real Conversation with God

The prayer of salvation is the most important prayer we'll ever pray. When we're ready to become a Christian, we're ready to have our first real conversation with God, and these are its components:

We acknowledge that Jesus Christ is God, that he came to earth as a man in order to live the sinless life that we cannot live, and that he died in our place so that we would not have to pay the penalty we deserve.

We confess our past life of sin, living for ourselves and not obeying God. We admit we are ready to trust Jesus Christ as our Savior and Lord. We ask Jesus to come into our heart, take up residence there, and begin living through us.

Prayer of Salvation: It Begins with Faith in God

When we pray the prayer of salvation, we're letting God know we believe his Word is true. By the faith He has given us, we choose to believe in Him. The Bible tells us that *without faith it is impossible to please Him, for he who comes to God must believe that He is, and that He is a rewarder of those who diligently seek Him* (Hebrews 11:6).

So when we pray, asking God for the gift of salvation, we're exercising our free will to acknowledge that we believe in Him. That demonstration of faith pleases God because we have freely chosen to know Him.

Prayer of Salvation: Confessing Our Sin

When we pray the prayer of salvation, we're admitting that we've sinned. As the Bible says of everyone, save Christ alone: "*For all have sinned, and fall short of the glory of God*" (Romans 3:23).

To sin is simply to fall short of the mark, as an arrow that does not quite hit the bull's-eye. The glory of God that we fall short of is found only in Jesus Christ:

> *For it is the God who commanded light to shine out of darkness, who has shone in our hearts to give the light of the knowledge of the glory of God in the face of Jesus Christ* (2 Corinthians 4:6).

The prayer of salvation, then, recognizes that Jesus Christ is the only human who ever lived without sin.

> *For He made Him who knew no sin to be sin for us, that we might become the righteousness of God in Him* (2 Corinthians 5:21).

~ Chapter 16 ~
Full Circle

Jesus replied, Very truly I tell you,
no one can see the kingdom of God
unless they are born again (John 3:3).

After a small publication and introduction to my business, I was contacted by another strong believer in faith. They were working to develop some community support initiatives and invited me to fly to Mobile, Alabama, to watch them speak. I knew it was right. I knew I must go. God called me.

Plus, that was the place of my birth, and I had always wanted to go back and look at the place where I was born and revisit—weird as it sounds—the place in my driveway where I had dropped a crowbar on my left big toe. I don't know why that was so important to me; likely because it was one of my first memories that I wanted to go back to.

Well, God took me there.

I committed to attending the meeting in Alabama with one of my team members and had the pleasure of visiting my hometown in spring 2019, roughly thirty-three years after we left.

I took an Uber to the old neighborhood while on the phone with my mom. It didn't seem like the right place because it didn't have a carport. She explained I was at our second house. We had another house before that one just down the street behind the elementary school.

The Uber driver was from the area and knew exactly where she was talking about, and he offered to take me there. I called my mom back once we pulled up in front of the house and texted her photos. She confirmed I was at the right place.

I asked the gentleman if I could have five minutes. Luckily no one was home. I stood in the exact spot from thirty years before. It filled me with glee. It made my heart happy. It took me home. My eyes welled with tears as I thought about the generosity God had blessed me with in my life. I immediately sent pictures to my siblings and mom and shared the experience with them.

I believe God took me full circle so I could restart, rebuild my story, and fill in gaps so I could begin to write because I've been dreaming of this book for years. When I was not following him, I didn't know anything about it. God called upon me to share my story so people could read these stories to clearly see that God is real.

God showed me how the book should be written. He told me in a vision what the cover of the book would be and how to get that completed. He described the inlay, the binding, and the various verses that should be laid out. He's instructed me about the dedication, how each story will hit a little place with each person. I pray that this is your moment. The moment in which you can see God working in your life. Take this moment, breathe it in, and let it catapult you into a deeper relationship with him.

I asked God how to close this book, and he led me to Isaiah 26.

We have a strong city; God makes salvation, its walls and ramparts.

Open the gates that the righteous nation may enter, the nation that keeps faith.

You will keep in perfect peace those whose minds are steadfast because they trust in you.

Trust in the Lord forever, for the Lord, the Lord himself, is the Rock eternal.

He humbles those who dwell on high, he lays the lofty city low; he levels it to the ground and casts it down to the dust.

Feet trample it down the feet of the oppressed, the footsteps of the poor.

The path of the righteous is level; you, the Upright One, make the way of the righteous smooth.

Yes, Lord, walking in the way of your laws, we wait for you; your name and renown are the desire of our hearts.

My soul yearns for you in the night; in the morning my spirit longs for you.

When your judgments come upon the earth, the people of the world learn righteousness.

But when grace is shown to the wicked, they do not learn righteousness; even in a land of uprightness they go on doing evil and do not regard the majesty of the Lord.

Lord, your hand is lifted high, but they do not see it.

Let them see your zeal for your people and be put to shame; let the fire reserved for your enemies consume them.

*Lord, **you establish peace for us;** all that we have accomplished you have done for us.*

Lord our God, other lords besides you have ruled over us, but your name alone do we honor.

They are now dead; they live no more; their spirits do not rise.

You punished them and brought them to ruin; you wiped out all memory of them.

You have enlarged the nation, Lord; you have enlarged the nation. *You have gained glory for yourself; you have extended all the borders of the land.*

Lord, they came to you in their distress; when you disciplined them, they could barely whisper a prayer.]

As a pregnant woman about to give birth writhes and cries out in her pain, so were we in your presence, Lord.

We were with child, we writhed in labor, but we gave birth to wind. We have not brought salvation to the earth, and the people of the world have not come to life.

*But your dead will live, Lord; their bodies will rise—***let those who dwell in the dust wake up and shout for joy***—your dew is like the dew of the morning; the earth will give birth to her dead.*

Go, my people, enter your rooms and shut the doors behind you; hide yourselves for a little while until his wrath has passed by.

See, the Lord is coming out of his dwelling to punish the people of the earth for their sins. The earth will disclose the blood shed on it; the earth will conceal its slain no longer (Isaiah 26:1–21).

Acknowledgements
(In no particular order)

To Wanda: thank you for always encouraging me to find my cheerleaders, to "do me," and for being such a strong inspiration watching you hustle.

To Toni: I miss you. COVID took you too soon. Thank you for bringing laughter. For teaching me how to live in the Joy God wants for us. For encouraging me to step out and be a CEO. For the times in Texas when we traveled for work that you wished cars out of our way on the freeway, and they moved. For how to cross out the bad luck from black cats. For the random scrambles for donuts and BBQ while traveling on the road. For helping me after my surgery: I could go on: but I'll wait until we meet again.

To Clay: thank you for the features, continued encouragement to me, and the business.

To David S.: appreciate your fervent prayers for us: we are seeing them be answered. I can only hope that we can fulfill his vision soon and work hard for his kingdom.

To Kathleen: thank you for helping me document my testimony and creating magic. You came into my life by the divine and are a miracle.

To Nancy: thank you for welcoming me to a new town, a new church, and for the banana bread: a little taste of God's glory here on earth.

To my husband: let's dance.

To my mother: Thank you for teaching me perseverance and overcoming circumstance. For getting me involved with horses, letting me drink out of the hose, and letting me pick clovers in the lawn. Not thankful for having to deliver papers in the snow in Ohio.

To my brother: not thankful for the lemon juice or opera music but thankful for you being there when I needed you.

To my sister: I hope you are well.

To my children: you are part of my journey. May God continue to keep you from all harm or pitfalls. May you never waiver in his love for you. Here's to the next generation's bountiful blessings.

To my nieces and nephews: You are brave, strong, and full of the power of Christ; lean on him each day. I love you and am so proud of each of you.

To Veronica: I would have never stepped foot in Church had it not been for you. You are the beginning: the seed and for that I am forever thankful. Keep advocating for Christ: and rest knowing you are a wonderful child of God.

To Ginny: Never in my life have I felt so much friendship, trust and selfless acts of hope and help you bring. I can't even put into words how much impact you have had in my spiritual walk to step out in faith. He is moving mountains. Thank you for trusting in me.

To Kate: You know, but to make sure you know. You are amazing woman. An epic mother and wife: they do not make them like you. Keep on pushing.

To Catherine: Thank you for teaching me how to pray softly. To remain faithful: for sharing the bible and plantains. My sister in Christ.

To Mary: thank you for your kindness, and for helping pave the path to our success.

To Pastor Paul: Thank you for preaching *is all well with your soul?* Had it not been for that sermon, I would not have written this.

To Aunt Missy: Thanks for being my sounding board. For driving me to and fro. For letting me sit and hang with you in your flower garden.

To Bob: Thank you for being there for me when I needed you the most. I miss you.

To my dad: You are an impeccable man. Thank you for passing down all the ideas, fruitful conversations, what if's, imagination, and laughter. Take your meds please.

To those that are not mentioned: Thank you for being a part of my life and helping to get me this moment. Your moment is now.

www.ingramcontent.com/pod-product-compliance
Lightning Source LLC
Chambersburg PA
CBHW021951090426
42811CB00041B/2405/J